A
YOUNG PERSON'S
GUIDE TO DRESSAGE

Jane Kidd

COMPASS EQUESTRIAN

LONDON

British Library Cataloguing in Publication Data
A catalogue record for this book is available from the British Library

ISBN 1 900667 55 X

Published in Great Britain in 1997 by
Compass Equestrian Limited
Eardley House
4 Uxbridge Street
Farm Place
London W8 7SY

Photographs by Kevin Sparrow and Jane Kidd
Line illustrations by Maggie Raynor
Illustration of Grand Prix Level Freestyle Test on page 15 reproduced with the permission of the FEI
Edited by Martin Diggle
Designed by Hugh Johnson
Printed and bound in Great Britain by
Biddles Ltd, Guildford and King's Lynn

CONTENTS

INTRODUCTION

Dressage has been good to me. It has been a source of many friends, provided opportunities for travelling around the world, and it has helped me to reach a better understanding of the horse, an animal who has always been central to my life. I have been absorbed by the unending challenges that this sport/art presents. I have enjoyed the artistic element and the opportunity for creativity. I have valued it as a way of developing discipline and responsibility; discipline being the outcome of paying attention to the detail needed in that tantalising search for perfection, and responsibility stemming from caring for another living creature. I have found it immensely satisfying to gain the trust of a naturally wild creature and to make him eager to work with me.

I would like more people to experience these pleasures and benefits. Because I know how easy it is to be put off by the apparent complexities of dressage and the mass of detail that appears to need mastering, this book focuses on what to aim for, and keeps the account of how to get there as simple and straightforward as possible. My aim is to 'get across' the excitement and challenges of the sport and not let you get too bogged down with technical detail. Once you are on the road and know where you are going, if there is a detail that needs filling in, you will find masses of books to help. Once you are 'hooked' on the sport there are many excellent, authoritative books to read.

My job then, is to make it clearer where to aim. If you do not have a clear picture of where you are going, you may end up back where you started! This is all too easy if you get *too* bogged down in the smaller details of 'how to do it'.

As a writer I have travelled extensively. I have seen the great riders and trainers at work and I have built up a clear picture of the trot I want from a young horse, and the way the transitions should look and feel. This has been a great advantage to me in dressage. In England one hears a great deal about what is wrong with the way a horse is going, where riders should put their hands, heads, and so on. This is all very useful detail, but that clear picture of the end product is so often missing.

In this book, I have tried to highlight the goals, and indicate as straight a path as possible towards them. I hope it will give you an overall picture of dressage, whet your appetite, and get you going.

I have aimed the book at the young, to whom this direct, clear approach usually appeals – who are often so much more successful than their seniors because they take no notice of the alternatives, the possibilities, the contingencies. Having no concept of the difficulties they think doing a flying change or a half-pass will be pretty easy, and therefore usually find it so. I hope, however, that the book will also appeal to all the young in mind (who could be as old as me!) – those who appreciate the same direct approach of youth and know that, later, they can fill in the detail, explore aspects in more depth – but first of all want a straightforward overall picture.

One final note here. I know many readers will have ponies, and I hope that they will not feel insulted because I have always used the term 'horse'. This does, technically, cover ponies – and it so much less cumbersome than saying 'horse or pony' all the way through the text.

CHAPTER 1
WHAT IS DRESSAGE?

Dressage is about controlling the power of the horse and giving the rider a chance to work in harmony with an animal who is much faster, stronger and more graceful than most of us could ever hope to be on our own two feet. It would be a form of dressage if we just brainwashed the horse into obedience: we would have trained him; but the real skill is in obtaining obedience through his willing co-operation, so that his spirit, his character and above all, his power and athleticism are maintained.

The aim in dressage is perfection – perfect natural movement, so that the wonderful, supple, flowing action which foals and youngsters display when playing free in the fields can be reproduced by our horses when we ride them. This is not so easy because, when you sit on top of a horse, you upset both his natural balance (because you make him carry your extra weight) and his mental state (because you take away some of his freedom and try to make him do what you want him to do).

Dressage may not be such an exciting sport as galloping across country, nor so thrilling as jumping a big course of show jumps, but there are some are wonderfully exhilarating moments, such as when your horse suddenly understands a movement that you are teaching him, or when he really uses his body and tries his hardest to produce a great extended trot. The other big attraction is that dressage is a never-ending challenge. Each day, you have to think of ways to help your horse – both mentally, to realise what you are seeking, and physically, to become more supple, more powerful, and more able to carry out the essential movements.

Whenever you train your horse you are doing a form of dressage, but over the centuries dressage riders have discovered that certain exercises will progressively make the horse a better partner – more obedient, more gymnastic, more able to do what is required of him. A series of dressage movements has thus been devised, and a progressive pattern has been developed. This takes the training from the very simple movements, such as coming to a halt, to the very difficult (both mentally and physically) like the canter pirouette, when the horse keeps cantering and, without going forward, turns through 360 degrees, or the piaffe, when the horse keeps trotting on the same spot. Any rider whose horse can be trained to piaffe or to pirouette in canter has a partner who is both enormously powerful and very obedient. These assets can be used for practical purposes – in the past they were used in mounted combat and for exotic displays in the courts of Europe. Today, they enable us to take part in competitions and hopefully win some trophies.

The pirouettes and piaffe are the most difficult dressage movements performed in competition. While beautiful to watch when done well, they also have practical value, as any horse who can do them should be a wonderful ride – light, responsive, manoeuvrable, powerful and very balanced. It takes considerable talent and years of training of horse and rider before they are able to do these movements well, but the great feature of dressage is that each movement taught brings benefits. When a horse can halt in balance he is going to be a safer and more pleasurable ride. When he can step sideways he is going to be more supple, more manoeuvrable. When he can keep his rhythm in canter even when shortening and extending his steps he is going to be much easier to ride into a fence.

All riders who want to make the most of their horses' natural talents – whether in show jumping, eventing, gymkhanas, showing or driving – will do some form of dressage, and the better the form the better the results. The more riders know about dressage and the more they make use of its principles, the better they will be at getting their horses to jump, go across country, gallop in races and turn in gymkhana events. Dressage is the basis of all equestrian sports, as it is simply the training of the horse.

Dressage helps horses to keep their balance and power in difficult situations like this one when jumping into water.

Thus every rider would be better off learning about dressage, but some do not want to use it merely as a means to end – to develop their show jumper's or eventer's talents – but as an end in itself, to compete in dressage competitions. Around the world there are more and more dressage competitions. Even in countries that have relatively few riders, such as India, Thailand and Malaysia, international events have started and, in some major countries like the USA and Britain, dressage is the fastest growing equestrian sport.

Dressage competitions are tests of the quality of the training. They are an assessment of how well the rider has managed to teach the horse the dressage movements. Tests are performed in an arena which is either 20 x 40 metres or 20 x 60 metres. Judges mark every movement out of 10, with each mark having a meaning – 10 being excellent (and rarely given!), 9 very good, 8 good, 7 fairly good, 6 satisfactory, 5 sufficient, 4 insufficient, 3 fairly bad, 2 bad, 1 very bad and 0 not executed.

There are also marks given at the end of the test for the general impression and the way of going of the horse – his paces, power and obedience. The general impression of the rider is not neglected; this also is given a special mark, and there is a space at the end of the test sheet where the judge can make comments about the rider's position, use of the aids and how much these helped the horse.

There are very simple tests for novice horses and very young riders. The easiest consist of nothing more difficult than to walk, trot and canter on both reins, to make some circles and to halt at the end. The tests then become progressively more difficult until they reach the ultimate level of competitive dressage – the Grand Prix. This is the test that decides who wins Olympic medals. It is in the Grand Prix that the trot on the spot – the piaffe – is included.

The harmony and power which epitomise top dressage. Olympic champions Isabell Werth and Gigolo have turned a powerful forward-going canter into one that can be maintained almost on the spot as they turn in a canter pirouette.

Key factors
* Dressage is a control of power, making the horse obedient and athletic.
* Dressage is simply training, and is the basis of all riding.
* The popularity of dressage is spreading, and it is the fastest growing equestrian sport in many countries.
* Dressage movements are designed to make the horse progressively more controllable and more gymnastic, so they range from very easy to very difficult; from Preliminary level to Grand Prix.
* The quality of the training is tested in competitions.

CHAPTER 2
WHO DOES DRESSAGE?

Any rider can do dressage – age is immaterial. Many of the top riders started very young, but no sport has so many older top riders. A 70-year-old, Lorna Johnstone, represented Britain at the Olympics. The German maestro, Dr Reiner Klimke, who has won more medals than any other rider, earned his first Olympic individual gold when he was 48, 24 years after he rode in his first Olympics. His debut in major championships was even earlier as he was only 19 when he competed at his first European Championships and, 40 years on, he is still winning international competitions. It is doubtful whether any other Olympic sport can give you the opportunity to stay in top competition for so long.

At the other end of the scale, Dominique d'Esmé, who won the team bronze for France at the 1995 European Championships, rode in her first Prix St Georges (an international level dressage test) when only 9 years old. The greatest partnership of our time, that of Nicole Uphoff-Becker from Germany and Rembrandt, was first formed when she was just 13 years old and he was 3. Eight years later, they were Olympic team and individual gold medallists.

There is no doubt that the young have one great advantage in dressage – they are much more supple and usually braver than older riders. They also have fewer hang-ups, are less aware of the consequences of taking a particular course of action, and so they simply head straight towards their goal. On the other hand, wisdom counts for much in dressage. The experience of training many horses helps in finding better ways of training others. So, as riders grow older and have to face the handicap of stiffening up, they can balance this defect with their greater knowledge. I remember that grand old lady Lorna Johnstone bemoaning the fact that 10 years after her Olympic appearance at 70 she was getting a bit stiff to teach her young Thoroughbred mare one-time flying changes.

Ultimately, then, dressage is a sport for all ages. It is also a sport which can bring satisfaction to riders throughout an extraordinary range of ability. To be a top rider calls for exceptional muscular control, great gymnastic ability and horsemanship, but it is also the only equestrian sport which can and has staged World Championships for the disabled. A person with severe handicaps can still train a horse to do some of the simpler movements, and a rider without legs can gain as much sense of achievment from getting the horse to trot and come back to walk when asked as an Olympic rider does from attaining a brilliant piaffe.

In dressage, riders and horses can find a level that suits their abilities and, if they perform better than others at this level – whether they are disabled, novice or young riders, on young horses, or international competitors, they can win prizes. In short, every rider can find an appropriate level and then have the goal of progressing to the next.

Some riders may be more limited by time than others. They might be unable or unwilling to spend hours each day doing dressage but, even if it is only a weekend sport or an occasional day in the week, there is satisfaction to be gained from progressing from one goal to the next – albeit more slowly than those who have more time available.

The great partnership of Nicole Uphoff-Becker and Rembrandt started when she was 13 and he was 3 years old. This is a study in concentration and focus as they work in before a major competition. But do not follow her example of not wearing a hat.

ORGANISING BODIES

To cater for the various levels of dressage, most countries have a system of organising bodies. These vary a little from one country to another, but all systems are progressive, and broadly along the lines of the British system described below.

THE PONY CLUB

The majority of young riders in Britain, USA, New Zealand and Australia get their first taste of dressage through the Pony Club. In Britain, nearly every area has a local Pony Club, and there are 368 branches nationwide. These give riders up to the age of 21 plenty of fun and education. There are individual Pony Club rallies, camps and competitions as well as inter-branch and Area competitions and National Championships.

RIDING CLUBS

In Britain, there are even more members of Riding Clubs than of the Pony Club, although the majority of members are adults. The Riding Clubs hold masses of dressage competitions and, like the Pony Club, there is a good range, starting with local and inter-club activities. The most prestigious competitions form a network of events leading up to the National

Championships and, at these, one day is devoted to competitions for riders under 21 who have qualified in team or individual events.

A young Pony Club rider preparing for her test.

NATIONAL ORGANISATION

Those who get 'hooked' on dressage, and want to take part in even more challenging events, can join the dressage branch of their National Federation. In Britain the National Federation is the British Equestrian Federation, and the dressage branch is the British Horse Society Dressage Group, which devises the tests, trains the judges, oversees the competitions and sends teams abroad.

The British range of tests starts at Preliminary level, then progresses through Novice, Elementary, Medium and Advanced Medium to Advanced. In the USA the range is from the Training Tests through First, Second, Third, Fourth and Fifth levels. An outline of the requirements and roughly equivalent levels are:

Test	Features
Preliminary/Training	Working paces, progressive transitions, circles.
Novice/Training	Lengthened strides, rein-back, counter-canter, 10m circles in trot, 15m circles in canter.
Elementary/1st level	Medium trot and canter, extended trot, shoulder-in, simple changes.
Medium/2nd Level	Collected walk, half pirouette, half-pass, extended walk, trot and canter.
Advanced Medium/3rd level	Flying changes, more collection.
Advanced/4th and 5th levels	Sequence changes, 6m volte (small circle), canter pirouettes.

INTERNATIONAL ORGANISATION

National Federations are members of the international organisation which is known as the Fédération Equestre Internationale (FEI). In all, the FEI is composed of 106 National Federations. It is the FEI that sets the standards, lays down the rules and provides the directives which all the major equestrian sports follow. For dressage there is the FEI Dressage Committee, whose rules and directives are published in a folder which is the 'bible' for the dressage world. Their directives lay down what the judges should look for, such as what the extended trot should look like and what 'on the bit' means.

The FEI also devises the tests for international competitions. The easiest of these is the Prix St Georges (Advanced/4th and 5th level), then the Intermediaire I and II and, ultimately, the Grand Prix and Grand Prix Special.

The FEI ensures that there are international championships each year. For senior riders this may be the Olympics (every fourth year), World Equestrian Games (every fourth year), European Championships or Pan American Games (every second year). For riders under 21 there are European Championships at three levels:

The Pony European Championships for riders between 12 and 16 years of age, riding ponies under 148cm (approx 14.2 hh).

The Junior European Dressage Championships for riders between 14 and 18 years.

The Young Rider European Dressage Championships for riders between 16 and 21 years.

The happiness of winning the gold medal and the title of Young Rider Individual Champion of Europe. Stefanie Schule from Germany thanks her horse Jozko.

The outline requirements for the various international tests are as follows:

Test	Features
Pony Rider Tests	Half-pass, simple changes, counter-canter, medium and extended paces.
Junior Tests	Single flying changes.
Young Rider Test	Sequence flying changes, half pirouettes in canter.
Prix St Georges	Three-and four-time changes, half pirouettes in canter.
Intermediaire I	Two-and three-time changes, full pirouettes.
Intermediaire II	Progressive piaffe, passage, 9 one-time changes.
Grand Prix	Piaffe and passage, 15 one-time changes.

Thus, in dressage there are plenty of opportunities for young riders to compete at every level from Pony Club through to international championships. For the very talented, very dedicated and very lucky there is the chance to become a European Champion.

FREESTYLE DRESSAGE TO MUSIC

One of the most exciting developments in dressage competitions has been the introduction of Freestyle to Music. The FEI approved the first international competition in 1979, and it was held at Goodwood, in England. The crowd loved this competition as it was fun to listen to and watch, and it was easy to appreciate which performers were the best, as they gave the impression of dancing in time to the music. The first major championship using this more artistic approach to dressage was the World Cup (started in 1985). Then, at the 1996 Olympics, the Freestyle to Music was included as one of the tests. The Olympic competitors had to prove that they had the flair to devise pleasing and orginal programmes, and they had to keep their horses working in time to the music. It was a great challenge for dressage competitors and a wonderful competition for spectators

Freestyle to Music is, however, pretty difficult for the judges, as they have to assess not only whether the rider performs the movements in a technically good manner, but also give what are known as the artistic marks. These are for: rhythm, energy and elasticity; harmony between rider and horse; choreography, use of arena, inventiveness; degree of difficulty and well-calculated risks; choice of music and interpretation of it.

Key factors

* Dressage competitors can be aged from 7 years to over 70.
* Any standard of rider can find a competition to suit.
* Pony Clubs, Riding Clubs and National Federations all run dressage competitions, and the FEI controls international dressage.
* Tests are a competitive form of dressage and they are grouped into grades, or levels. The higher the grade, the more difficult the test movements.
* There are Championships for riders under 21 as well as for senior riders.
* Tests to music are an exciting new form of competition.

A popular variation of the Freestyle is the Pas de Deux: this is the winning pair at the European Championships.

FEDERATION
EQUESTRE
INTERNATIONALE

Freestyle Test
(Grand Prix Level)

Time allowed:
Performance to be finished between 5'3'' and 6'.

Edition 1986
Rev. January 1995

Event	Date	Judge and position	No. in progr.		Competitor	Nation	Horse		No.	

	Technical marks	Marks	Points	Coeff.	Final Marks		Artistic marks	Marks	Points	Coeff.	Final Marks
1.	Collected walk (minimum 20 m)	10				16.	Rhythm, energy and elasticity	10		3	
2.	Extended walk	10				17.	Harmony between rider and horse	10		3	
3.	Collected trot including Half pass to the right	10				18.	Choregraphy. Use of arena. Inventivness	10		4	
4.	Collected trot including Half pass to the left	10				19.	Degree of difficulty. Well calculated risks.	10		4	
5.	Extended trot	10				20.	Choice of music and interpretation of the music	10		6	
6.	Collected canter including Half pass to the right	10					Total for artistic presentation	200			
7.	Collected canter including Half pass to the left	10									
8.	Extended canter	10					**To be deducted**				
9.	Flying changes of leg every second stride (minimum 5 times consecutively)	10					Time penalty: more than 6' or less than 5'30'' deduct 2 points from the total of artistic presentation				
10.	Flying changes of leg every stride (minimum 5 times consecutively)	10					**Score** (see conversion table)				
11.	Canter pirouette to the right	10		2			Total for technical execution divided by 20		10		
12.	Canter pirouette to the left	10		2			Total for artistic presentation divided by 20		10		
13.	Passage (minimum 20 m)	10		2							
14.	Piaffe (minimum 10 steps)	10		2			**Final score**		20		
15.	Transitions from passage to piaffe and from piaffe to passage	10		2			In case two competitors have the same final score, the one with the higher marks for artistic impression is leading.				
	Total for technical executions	200									
	Remarks										
	Signature of Judge										

Test sheet for Freestyle to Music.

CHAPTER 3
A BRIEF HISTORY OF DRESSAGE

DRESSAGE IN ANCIENT TIMES

Although chariot racing was the first equestrian sport to be part of the Olympics (way back in 676BC), dressage has the longest history of the current Olympic sports. It started more than 2,000 years ago and, in Classical times, the Greeks practised it to a high standard. The famous Parthenon frieze shows horses doing the movement which is the aim of all ambitious dressage riders today – the piaffe.

Certainly, the Greeks produced one of the great horsemen of all time in Xenephon (430–354BC), a cavalry commander who wrote the book *On the Art of Horsemanship*. This contains much advice that is still relevant today. One such piece is the section that explains the basis for all dressage. It is very simple and, perhaps because of that, it is all too often glossed over:

> The gods have given the power of instructing each other in their duties by word of mouth which is denied to a horse. But if you can reward him when he obeys as you wish and punish him when he is disobedient he will thus learn to know his duty.

In the centuries following the period in which the Greeks lost their domination of the civilized world to the Romans, the horse was used mainly as a practical conveyance in war, transportation, hunting, and for general work. Beyond basic training to make the horse better at performing these tasks, there is no evidence of dressage.

RENAISSANCE DRESSAGE

The revival of more advanced dressage came during the Renaissance when the rational approach that transformed art and literature was also applied to riding. This process began in Italy – the birthplace of the Renaissance – and the leader was the Neapolitan nobleman Frederico Grisone, who founded a riding academy in Naples in 1532. Here, Grisone demonstrated how reason and logic could be used to teach horses complicated movements, and instructed young noblemen in the art. The idea caught on. It was thought to be a good education for young men, and beneficial for their character, to learn how to train horses in this way. Those who became good at the art attained considerable prestige. To control horses in slow, dramatic paces; to be able to teach them spectacular movements; to make them dance to music – such skills earned a rider many admirers, and ambitious young men were keen to learn the techniques to help them further their careers.

Soon, dressage displays became popular court activities, and many young men travelled to Naples to learn how to make better use of their horses. As a result of this influx of foreign students, and because many Italian instructors travelled abroad, an understanding of the art of dressage began to spread across Europe.

DRESSAGE COMES TO ENGLAND

During his reign, Henry VII had ordered that any horse he had to ride on a state occasion was to be starved for 24 hours; this, rather than training, was his way of establishing control. However his successor, Henry VIII, heard about and embraced Grisone's more scientific approach. He employed Robert Alexander, a pupil of the Grisone school, and equitation was promoted as an honourable occupation at Hampton Court.

The greatest British master of dressage was William Cavendish, Duke of Newcastle. A tutor of Charles II, he was forced into exile when Cromwell destroyed the monarchy, and he set up an academy in Antwerp. His great book *A General System of Horsemanship* was published in 1658, and this was to influence many people, including Gustav Steinbrecht, a famous riding master in the nineteenth century – and the biggest influence on the German school. His book *The Gymnasium of the Horse*, published in 1885, is probably one of the most important in the history of dressage.

Through this connection, the British have played a small, if distant, part in the most successful school of modern dressage. However, the Duke of Newcastle sadly had little influence on British riders, who preferred racing and hunting to dressage, and it was France who took over from Italy as the nursery of the sport.

DRESSAGE IN FRANCE

It was two pupils of Grisone, Solomon de La Broue and Antoine de Pluvinel de Baume, who returned to France and started a fashion for dressage which lasted from the seventeenth to the nineteenth century. De Pluvinel taught Louis XIII and, after him, Louis XIV – who became even more enthusiastic about dressage, making his court at Versailles the centre for this increasingly fashionable activity. He was fortunate that during his reign the most famous riding master of all time, François Robichon, Sieur de la Guérinière, was teaching in Paris. It was he who laid down many of the principles that we still practise today. De la Guérinière wrote of dressage that:

> this noble and useful art...is solely to make horses supple, loose, flexible, compliant and obedient and lower the quarters without all of which a horse – he may be meant for military service, hunting or dressage – will be neither comfortable in his movements, nor pleasurable to ride.

Among his many achievements, de la Guérinière devised the movement of shoulder-in and developed counter-canter and the flying change. He designed a saddle which allowed the leg to hang ready to be applied, instead of stretched slightly forward. He also wrote the book *Ecole de Cavalerie*, which is still the guide for the most famous dressage school of modern times – the Spanish Riding School in Vienna.

CLASSICAL RIDING SCHOOLS

THE SPANISH RIDING SCHOOL

The Spanish Riding School was started after the Hapsburg court of Austria imported some Spanish horses in 1572. They chose these horses because they were particularly suitable for dressage, the activity so fashionable in all the major courts of Europe. These horses were used to develop a breed which was named the Lipizzaner after the stud of Lipica (now part of Slovenia) where they were based. More than four centuries later, the school still demonstrates top-class dressage in wonderful displays at its base in Vienna, and travels the world to show off its art. The Spanish Riding School is considered to be a custodian of history, and guardian of the art of classical riding.

THE CADRE NOIR

Neither so old nor so famous as the Spanish Riding School, but still very important, is the school at Saumur in France which is known as the Cadre Noir. In contrast to the Spanish Riding School, which uses grey horses for displays, the Cadre Noir uses black or brown horses, and the riders wear black uniforms. The name is therefore appropriate. The Cadre Noir took over as guardians of French dressage after the French Revolution destroyed the monarchy, and the many high-class riding masters who joined the troop helped develop dressage throughout the nineteenth century. In the twentieth century the Cadre Noir has produced some top dressage competitors, and still gives spectacular displays.

THE CIRCUS AND RUSSIA

The two most famous nineteenth-century riding masters in France were both circus riders. François Baucher was able to train a horse to perform spectacular movements − including trotting and cantering backwards − in record time. He was a great influence on riding in the mid-nineteenth century. However, James Fillis, an Englishman by birth, but brought up in France, had the more lasting influence. Some of this was in France but, in Russia, his methods became the basis of their successful dressage. (In 1972 the Russians won the Olympic team gold medal, becoming the only nation to beat the Germans in the last 30 years.)

   At the end of the nineteenth century, Fillis went to St Petersburg and the methods he wrote about in *Principes de Dressage et d'Equitation* were adopted by this country of great horsemen and wonderful, high-spirited horses.   The Russians became masters of collection and in twentieth-century competitions, showed brilliant piaffe, passage, and pirouettes − although they did lose marks on the basic work − the quality of the paces; the walk, trot and canter. The Russian methods, influenced by Fillis, produced spectacular movements but failed to nurture the natural talent of the horse; the brilliance of the paces that is thought so important in modern competitions.

   British attitudes towards dressage are highlighted by the fact that Fillis's book *Principes de Dressage et d'Equitation* was called *Breaking and Training* in its English version, and even the 1990 edition had this misleading translation. Publishers thought that the British would not buy a book with 'dressage' in the title!

DRESSAGE AS A SPORT

Throughout the period from the sixteenth to the nineteenth century, dressage was used for displays, as good education for young noblemen, and to help train cavalry. It was not until the twentieth century that it was turned into a competitive sport. The first major event was at the 1912 Olympics in Stockholm, when equestrian sports were included for the first time since the Classical Greek era. The dressage test, which focused on obedience, included five small jumps, and there were spooky objects to be passed. However, the test soon became more sophisticated and, by the 1930s it contained all the movements which are included in modern Olympic tests − piaffe, passage and one-time changes.

The major change to dressage in recent years has been its huge increase in popularity, especially amongst young people. With so many people taking up the sport it has become worthwhile for breeders to produce stock specifically for dressage. This has led to more talented horses, and a trend towards a finer, more elegant type. The general standard of dressage riding has also improved as more ambitious people have taken it up and been willing to dedicate their lives to becoming top-class dressage riders.

Alongside this increase in the grace and quality of horses and riders has been the advent of a more artistic form of dressage – the Freestyle to Music. These factors all contribute to the sport becoming more and more beautiful to watch.

Experts in Freestyle: *Anky van Grunsven and Bonfire, who have been World Champions at this new form of competitive dressage.*

Key dates

4th Century BC: Xenophon rode and wrote in Athens.

1532: Federico Grisone founds Naples Riding Academy.

1572: Spanish Riding School of Vienna founded.

16th Century: Dressage comes to England with the support of Henry VIII.

1623: Publication of *Manège Royal* by Antoine de Pluvinel .

1666: Publication of *General System of Horsemanship* by the Duke of Newcastle.

1730-1751: De la Guérinière Master of the Stables of Louis XIV.

1733: Publication of de la Guérinière's *Ecole de Cavalerie*.

1874: Publication of *Methode d'Equitation* by Francois Baucher.

1885: Publication of *Gymnasium of the Horse* by Gustav Steinbrecht.

1890: Publication of *Principes de Dressage et d'Equitation* by James Fillis.

1898: Fillis appointed Chief Instructor to the Russian Cavalry Officers School at St Petersburg.

1912: Dressage included in Olympic Games at Stockholm.

CHAPTER 4
GETTING STARTED

PRELIMINARY REQUIREMENTS

There are two basics that need to be tackled before a rider can help, rather than hinder, the horse when doing dressage. The first is to establish a good posture on the horse, and to be able to stay in balance with him. This is relatively easy if the rider is taught correctly from the start so that bad habits never develop. Research has shown that to get out of a bad habit a rider has to do the action correctly 2,000–3,000 times. To avoid going through this painstaking procedure, it is well worth focusing on establishing a good position from the start! The easiest way of achieving this is on the lunge, through voltige (horseback vaulting) and by working under the eye of a good teacher.

It is work like this on the lunge that helps the rider to develop a balanced position.

The second basic requirement is to get to understand horses by finding out how their minds work. They cannot be treated like machines, nor like humans, as they have very good memories but do not reason. A dressage rider must realise that when a horse does not obey this is rarely because of stubborness or being in a bad mood, but because he does not understand.   An important part of dressage is to learn how to give horses confidence; to build up communication, trust and respect.

Understanding horses comes from working with them, looking after them in stables and the field, feeding them to suit their temperament and condition, and riding them in a variety of circumstances. Those who feel brave enough to go across country, or to try some show jumping or gymkhanas find that these are tremendous ways of helping to build up a better understanding of horses.

The extent to which these two qualities are present in a newcomer to dressage will be somewhat dependent upon previous riding experience. A rider who has already had plenty of experience of other equestrian sports, such as hunting, eventing, show jumping or even polo, should be able to bypass some of the early dressage lessons, especially those related to building up an understanding of the horse.

THE STARTING POINTS

FINANCE

How a dressage rider gets going does depend on the starting point. It could be that the family has no money to spend on horses and training. But there is no need to be disheartened. It is quite possible to work for rides – mucking out stables, rolling up bandages, cleaning tack and suchlike and, when leaving school, going to join a top yard. This is the way British international Jane Bredin started, working for David Hunt as a groom, learning about the sport and ending up riding for Britain.

Working for rides is the way in which many (including the very best British team riders such as Emile Faurie, Carl Hester and Ferdi Eilberg) have achieved success, so lack of money is not a handicap so long as you are determined and hard-working. It is amazing how far enthusiasm can take you in dressage.

However, if you are lucky enough to have a family who can afford to buy horses and finance your riding, then make the most of it. The Barcelona Olympic champion Nicole Uphoff-Becker had good horses bought for her and was given good training by her family – but it was her dedication and love of the sport which allowed her to maximise these opportunities.

The first consideration, then, is money. As with most projects, preparing a budget makes clearer which path to take. A top-class international dressage pony or a talented schoolmaster horse could cost tens of thousands of pounds, lessons with a top trainer perhaps £50 a time, and keeping a horse at a competition livery yard up to £130 a week. If you can afford to take this high road it does, of course, have advantages, but for the majority it is out of the question.

If you can take the middle road, you can buy an unproven youngster, or an old schoolmaster past his best for between £2,000 and £5,000. Alternatively, you can lease a well-trained horse and use young, less expensive trainers, or take group lessons. Especially in the case of ponies, many of the best are never sold on, because the family has become too fond of them. When they are outgrown they are often available on loan or lease to a good home.

If you are unable to afford your own horse, you can work in exchange for rides, borrow horses, or ride for others. With the right commitment, any of these roads can lead to success.

This pony would be expensive as he has won the German Championship for three-year-olds.

This horse was not so expensive. He was bought young and is a British part bred, but with good training he went on to represent Britain on the Junior team.

WHERE TO KEEP YOUR OWN HORSE

The second consideration is not just the money but the feasibility of keeping a horse at home. Doing this requires knowledge, facilities, time and a very responsible approach. These, and other relevant matters, are dealt with in detail in The Learning Options (below).

If keeping a horse at home is at least a possiblity, the decision about whether to do so may be partly dependent upon what schools and training yards there are in your area. If they are either non-existent or second rate, then the option of keeping the horse at home may require more consideration. However, if the prospects are good, there is much to be said for doing your dressage with others: it is usually more fun, and a quicker way of learning.

THE LEARNING OPTIONS

A RIDING SCHOOL

This is a good way to start if the school is run by knowledgeable people who provide suitable horses. It is important to check that the school is licensed by the local authority (which is a legal requirement), and it should also be approved by the British Horse Society and/or be a member of the Association of British Riding Schools. Preferably, the school should also have an active interest in dressage, with a record of pupils competing.

THE HORSE AT HOME

For any horse-lover there is little to beat the chance of being able to go and see your own horse and take care of him before and after school or work. However, there are important points to consider if you are able to choose this option:

1) Awareness of the responsibilities of taking care of a horse. These are huge, and include the necessity for daily attention, knowledge of feeding, stabling, veterinary care etc.

2) Getting the right horse. The quickest way of learning is on a schoolmaster who knows how to do what you want to learn. Trying to train a horse when you yourself are learning is a much slower process, and can be hazardous. It is also important to choose a horse of appropriate size, with a sensible, co-operative temperament, and one whom a vet has tested as sound. He should also have a balanced and correct make and shape and good, rhythmic paces. If parents or friends are not qualified to help with your selection, recruit a suitably experienced adviser.

3) As you advance in dressage, facilities become increasingly important. In the early stages, a relatively flat area in a grass field is sufficient but, when you start to compete, an arena of 20 x 40 metres (later, 20x60 metres) is needed to practise the tests. The surface is also important because if it is slippery or muddy it will be difficult to keep a rhythm, and if it is hard the horse will get jarred and lose elasticity. Therefore, it becomes essential to have either very good old turf or an artificial surface within riding distance.

4) Progress in dressage is dependent upon getting good and consistent advice. Parents who are good riders themselves can help to keep you on the right path, but it is usually worthwhile geting some expert instruction. This will help prevent you from developing bad habits.

Young horses are likely to be mischievous when they first discover the excitement of shows. They need experienced, brave riders — so do not buy one until you are well prepared.

GOING TO A DRESSAGE YARD

With dressage booming in so many countries there are more and more competition yards around. Often owners or managers of these are keen to get help and, in exchange, they will sometimes offer some riding or, at least, allow helpers to watch the training.

Before offering to help, it is important to check on the reputation of the yard and establish that the training is done along classical lines.

Remember that helpers who are enthusiastic and hard-working are much more likely to be given opportunities. In the beginning, you will often have to prove your keenness by accepting and doing menial tasks willingly.

It may be that a mixture of the options outlined is suitable – perhaps keeping a young horse at home and getting lunge lessons at a riding school, or riding a schoolmaster at the riding school and working at a competition yard where you can watch the training. Just keep in mind that the first stage in dressage is to focus on the two basics – acquiring a good position and learning to understand horses. Use whatever means are available in order to achieve these goals.

John Lassetter's yard at Goodwood has a great reputation for helping young riders. These three have all competed internationally on horses from his stables.

Helping with the mucking out can get you some rides.

ADDITIONAL WAYS OF LEARNING
Watching
Working under instruction is the most obvious way of learning dressage but there are plenty of other things that can help. One of the first lessons to be learnt in dressage is the value of watching – not superficial looking, but concentrated studying. It is amazing what improvements can be made by simply watching good riders, and this is even more effective if you imagine you are riding the horse as you watch what is going on.(Remember, however, that while watching good riders can have a positive influence on your riding, watching bad riders can encourage the development of bad habits – so choose who you watch with care.)

Watching to learn can be done in so many places: at shows (especially in the riding-in area); in training yards; at Pony Club events and by looking at the ever-increasing number of videos about dressage.

In Britain, we take our young riders abroad, to the German National Training Centre at Warendorf, and to watch the best competitors at the famous German show at Aachen. Without riding a single horse, or having any instruction, all those who go on these trips return able to ride better.

Watching other riders having lessons is also beneficial, because then you can both watch and listen to what the instructor is saying. In most countries there is an increasing number of clinics being given by top trainers and, even if you are not advanced enough in your riding or wealthy enough to have a lesson, you can learn much from going along and studying. It is also fun to go with friends and exchange views about what you see.

Watching can lead on to other benefits. Ferdi Eilberg, who rides for Britain, started his career with horses as a groom. In his lunch hour, he would go and watch the great champion Reiner Klimke school his horses. After weeks of this the great rider was so impressed by such interest that he asked Ferdi to walk one of his horses to cool off. Following this, Ferdi was allowed to loosen horses up at the start of a session, and eventually he was offered a job. So enthusiastic watching gave Ferdi – a future silver medallist – his big break.

Being with other enthusiasts is stimulating and usually provides opportunities for learning, so it can be a good idea to join groups where this might happen. It could be the local Pony Club, Riding Club or Regional Dressage Group. Some research into what is a thriving dressage organisation in your area may be useful.

Working with others
Dressage is a sport in which you can have more fun and make quicker progress if you are training with others. It helps to be able to discuss problems with others and to question their methods of training. It also helps to have someone watching and commenting on what you are doing, and it is a big inspiration to ride with people who are more experienced than you and who sit better. So, even if you have your own arena at home, seize any opportunity to ride at a school, training yard, Pony Club or group activity – wherever there are other dressage enthusiasts around.

EQUIPMENT

In the early stages all that is needed is a hard hat to protect your valuable head, and some form of trousers that will not wrinkle, rub your legs, and make it more difficult to establish a relaxed, balanced position. However, well-fitting jodhpurs and boots are a sensible choice. For those who are older and taller, breeches and boots or half chaps are even better – and it does help you to keep still in the saddle if the seat of your breeches is made of synthetic material or leather, which tends to stick rather than slip.

Gloves are a good idea (indeed, they *must* be worn for tests) but for general riding they need only be very cheap, woollen ones with little bubbles of rubber on the inside to help grip the reins.

A long dressage whip does help when it comes to training a horse, as it can be used to reinforce a leg aid without having to take the hand off the rein.

Spurs are important as the training advances, but are not needed in the beginning.

A good saddle does help in the establishment of that crucial balanced position, and a good saddle does not mean a 'dressage saddle' with straight flaps and a deep seat that the salesman says will keep you in a good position. You must establish a position through balance, not because you are being held in place. I prefer saddles with flatter seats as these tend to sit on the horse better, do not shift around so much on the back, and distribute the rider's weight over a larger area, so it is easier for the horse to bear. It is important for the rider to be comfortable, and it is in both the rider's and horse's interests to ensure the horse is equally comfortable. If he is pinched, rubbed or has the rider's weight distributed unevenly, he will stiffen and move awkwardly – which will make it more difficult for the rider to stay relaxed. Any general-purpose saddle which fits you and the horse well is a sensible start for dressage.

The bridle must be of strong, sound leather or synthetic fibre, and does not need to be fancy and expensive. The aim in dressage is to ride novice horses in a snaffle, and a loose ring one is the best for getting that nice, elastic feel with the mouth. An eggbut, fixed ring snaffle is useful for those horses who do not take the contact.

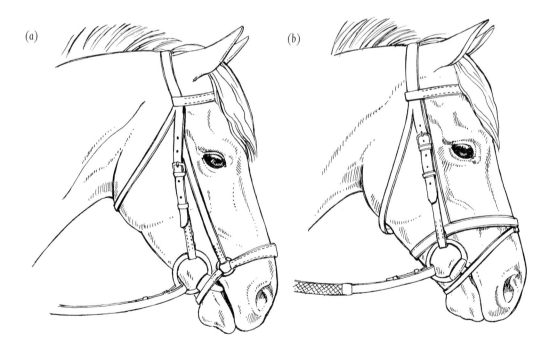

(a) *Poorly fitting bridle with a bit that is too wide and too low in the mouth. The browband is too small and the drop noseband is slightly low and might restrict the breathing.*
(b) *Well-fitting bridle with the bit high enough to wrinkle the sides of the mouth but not to pull it up. The flash noseband and the rubber reins are popular among dressage riders.*

Saddle types and fitting.

(b) This saddle is rather high but although this makes the saddle less secure it causes less damage than when the pommel is so low that it hits the wither.

Care must be taken that the saddle fits comfortably over the horse's shoulders. In (a) there is a danger that the tree points could be digging into the horse.

(a) This saddle is clearing the wither with ease.

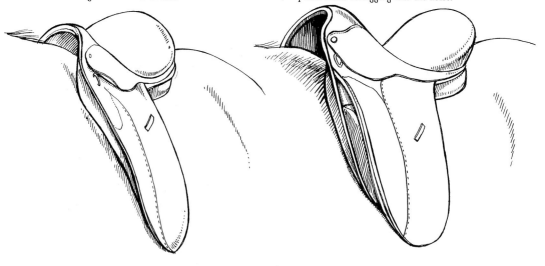

(c) The method of checking whether the pommel is clearing the withers

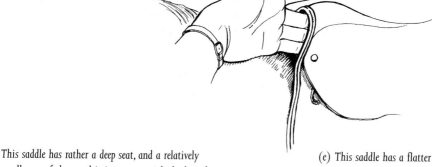

(d) This saddle has rather a deep seat, and a relatively small area of the panel is in contact with the horse's back. The rider's weight will be concentrated onto a small part of the back.

(e) This saddle has a flatter seat and a bigger area in contact with the horse's back. This means the weight-bearing area is larger, and reduces the risk of damage to the horse.

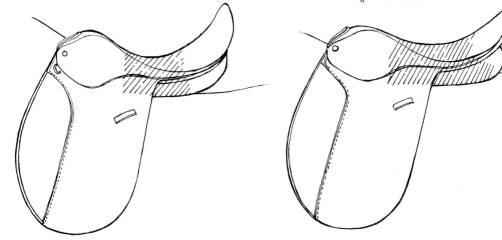

In the first stages of learning about dressage, it is crucial to develop good hands and not to pull back against the horse. If the horse is strong, this will be very difficult. So, although you must take care not to over-bit the horse (as this will make him nervous and over-sensitive to the rein aids) with some tough, older horses and ponies, it might be helpful to use a double-jointed snaffle or pelham in the early stages (but check the rules if you want to use them in competition, as they are not allowed at some levels).

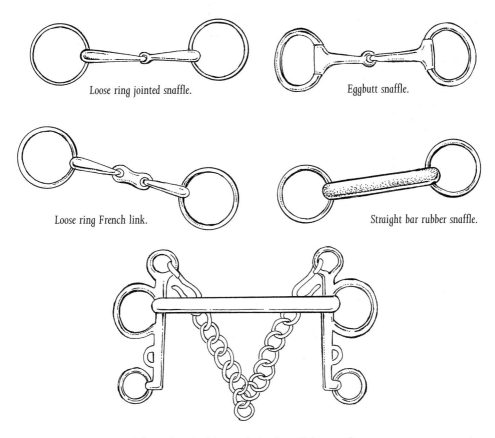

Loose ring jointed snaffle.

Eggbutt snaffle.

Loose ring French link.

Straight bar rubber snaffle.

Pelham. Permitted in some junior Pony Club tests only.

Various types of bit.

Key Factors
* The importance of establishing a good position, and understanding the mind of the horse.
* Your course of action will depend upon money, opportunites at home, opportunities locally, and the standard of your riding.
* The main options are using a riding school, having a horse at home, and/or going to a dressage yard.
* Watching is a very useful way of learning.
* Working with others is beneficial in dressage.

CHAPTER 5
THE KEY – A BALANCED POSITION

A good position enables you to stay in balance with the horse, remaining poised and supple, becoming 'part of the horse's movement'. It does not mean a seat where you stiffen up in order to do everything you have been told: keep the legs still, the elbows close to the body, the heels down and the like. Novice riders should be wary of *trying hard* to keep the hands, legs, hips, etc. where the text books say. This 'trying' introduces tension, which will make it more difficult to keep in tune with the horse's movement. The technically correct places for the shoulders, hands etc. are the refinements, and most will fall into place naturally when you are balanced and upright. If there are problems, these can be focused on at a more advanced stage.

A balanced, upright seat which is so important if horse and rider are to understand each other and work in harmony.

WHY IT IS WORTH DEVELOPING A GOOD SEAT

A balanced, upright seat is much more important in dressage than in any other equestrian sport. When jumping and galloping across country, the rider has to alter position when coming into a fence, when in the air and when galloping on the flat. If the positions are not balanced this will not be helpful to the horse, but because the weight is not being carried constantly on the same area of the horse's back — as it is in dressage — it will not do so much damage to the back.

The problem when the rider's weight is not central is that the horse will tend to move in order to be underneath the weight. If the rider's weight is more on the left than the right side, the horse will drift to the left and the rider will tend to start pulling on the right rein to keep him straight (see illustration (a) below). Two aids (weight and reins) will be in use before even starting to make the horse do anything. With so many messages coming to him, the horse will be confused, and will become increasingly insensitive. In addition to this pretty serious ill effect, the long-term carrying of an uneven weight leads to uneven muscular development. As a result, the horse will start to move unevenly and could even become lame.

Any shift in weight on a trained dressage horse has an enormous effect. If you work under a trainer with a schoolmaster and you try a leg-yield or half-pass, the trainer might ask you to put a little more weight on one seat bone and — hey presto — the horse, from struggling sideways, will flow fluently across. Because a dressage horse is very sensitive to weight positioning, weight effects can be used positively to help him do his work, or negatively to make it more difficult. If the positioning of the weight is not under the rider's control it is likely to hinder the horse's movement.

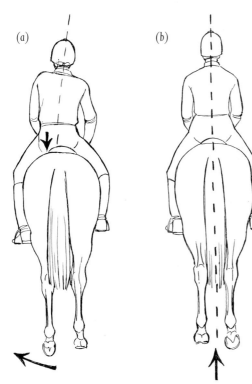

(a) The rider's weight has fallen to the left and the horse will tend to drift left.
(b) The rider's weight is balanced and evenly distributed, which will make it easy for the horse to go straight.

Distribution of weight.

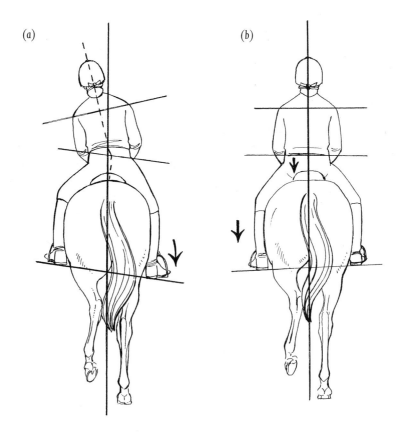

(a) (b)

Use of weight.
(a) The rider has leant to the left to apply the weight aid. The result is a loss of the upright position, with the seat slipping to the right. The effect will tend to be the opposite to that intended as the weight will drift to the right.
(b) The weight has been correctly applied onto the left seat bone and foot and the upright position maintained.

The unbalanced rider is a handicap to the aim of making the horse more athletic. If, in addition, the rider's weight bumps up and down, the horse is bound to start stiffening against it. Therefore the rider has to be supple enough to move with the horse, allowing the flow of the movement because he is relaxed.

Try this for yourself with a friend. Get down on all fours and ask someone to sit on you with their weight on one side and find out about the adjustments you have to make to stay balanced. Find out too how, when the weight bumps up and down on your back and does not stay in constant contact, you hollow away from it and become tight and tense.

FIRST AIMS

1) To be supple, able to carry yourself with poise and without twists or bends in your spine when you are off the horse. You cannot hope to keep straight when a horse is moving if you cannot sit straight in a chair or stand with poise. Neither can you absorb the movement of the horse if you are stiff when still on the ground.

2) To focus on the straightforward key factors in developing a balanced seat; namely awareness of the seat bones and remaining upright.

3) To be aware that a good seat is catching. Riding with others who have good positions, watching them at shows and on video, is a very effective way of getting a good position.

Keeping an upright position even when the pony's weight goes onto his forehand. Many riders would have been pulled forward, which would have made the pony even more unbalanced.

WORK OFF THE HORSE

It is much cheaper, less damaging to the horse and usually quicker to work on becoming supple and poised when on the ground. Very few people are absolutely straight. School work usually aggravates any problem because leaning on the desk, with the pen hand more forward than the other, develops a slouch and a twist that soon become habits difficult to cure. This will make it difficult to be straight when riding, and is likely to lead to back pain in the future. So, for the sake of your riding and the prevention of future pain, learn to stand and sit with your back erect and your weight evenly distributed on both feet/buttocks.

When you are fairly young, this straightness is readily achievable by thinking about posture and listening to comments from your parents! When they say 'sit up' or 'stand up straight', try not to blow a fuse because, although aggravating, it is in your own interests. If it does prove too difficult to get straight on your own, explore the Alexander Technique, which is being used by more and more riders. This helps you to become straight and poised.

So far as suppleness is concerned most exercises will help, but the areas to focus on are:

1) Stretching. Aim to get the legs and the spine as long as possible, and to become as tall as possible. To achieve this: touch your toes; stand on tip-toe and, with arms stretched above your head, run on the spot; hang from beams.

2) Loosening the joints and strengthening the muscles in the legs, so that hips, knees and ankles move freely. Leg bends, keeping your feet flat on the floor and taking your bottom closer to the floor, help to achieve this – and are useful to master as they make it much easier to oil horse's hooves and to do up boots!

3) Loosening and strengthening the lower back. Use sit-ups; lie flat on the floor and allow

your spine to fall back so that it is in contact with the floor – even where it hollows naturally around the waist.

4) Loosening the shoulders. These areas are full of tension, and are often hunched up and/or slightly twisted. Shrug them up and down, put your hands on the points and take them forwards and backwards.

FOCUSING ON THE SEAT BONES

These are the points that take most of your weight and, when this falls correctly, provide the base for a balanced seat. (Correctly speaking, the seat is three-point; the other part in contact with the saddle being that part of the pelvis between, and in front, of the seat bones, known as the crotch. However, this does not have such a definite contact as the seat bones, and most people find the two seat bones quite enough to focus on.)

The two seat bones should:

Rest on the lowest part of the saddle – neither on the slope from the cantle nor the slope from the pommel, but on the flattest area. Positioning them here will make it easier to remain stable.

Bear equal amounts of the weight. As your riding advances, shifting your weight from one seat bone to another will be one of the most useful aids, but the first stage is to be able to establish an even contact through each seat bone, and this is not so easy. Sometimes it will be very difficult to feel one of the seat bones at all, so here is an exercise you can do. Starting with the horse standing still, shift around, putting all your weight on one seat bone, then on the other. Lean forwards and backwards, swing your legs around, then grow taller until you are in a position where you can feel both seat bones evenly. It might feel odd, but this is the sensation to hang on to. Keep those seat bones touching the saddle, acting like suction pads, and with an even feel in both – this is the key to getting balanced.

Be equally placed either side of the centre line of the saddle, and at right angles to it. If there is any tendency to collapse your body on one side, then the seat bones will move across away from the side of the collapse. If one leg is stronger than the other, then one seat bone will tend to be further forward than the other. For example, in right-handed people who have a stronger right leg, the right seat bone will keep drifting forward.

If necessary, wriggle around to get your seat bones central. When riding with stirrups take care to put equal weight in both stirrup irons. When rising to the trot, rise evenly off both legs.

So get those seat bones in a comfortable position in the saddle, keep the weight evenly distributed on them, and keep them central. One of my most vivid memories of the teaching in Germany was the lessons for the young. For most of the lesson, and for day after day, few commands were given other than 'sitzen', 'sitzen', 'sitzen'.

FOCUSING ON BEING UPRIGHT

Of course there is a danger, when you focus on keeping your seat bones in the saddle that you may sit very heavily on the horse, but the answer to this is that keeping the seat bones glued to the saddle needs to be combined with an upright posture. So your back should be stretched upwards, and neither hollowed nor slouched. The stretching should be achieved without stiffening, and I have found that the best image for getting the right effect is: 'Imagine that you are bouncing a ball on the top of your head'. This encourages the rider to stretch upwards frequently, without tightening. Take care that when you stretch upwards you do not raise your shoulders. If you do this they will have to tighten to be held in this unnatural position. Preferably, the upward stretch should be along the spine to the top of the head.

In addition to stretching upwards away from the seat bones so that the back is poised and upright, it is also necessary to stretch downwards, so that your legs hang like damp, clammy towels around the horse's sides.

If you can keep your seat bones correctly placed in the saddle and remain upright, you will be balanced. If you can do these things when your horse is trotting and cantering, you are well on your way to establishing a good position.

Quiet hands are very important and should be held as if carrying mugs. These are in a pretty good position, but just a little too high to get that straight line from the elbow to the bit.

GETTING SUPPLE

When you are balanced it will be much easier to let go and relax the muscles that allow your body to absorb the horse's movement. But remember, it is also easier to be balanced when you are supple and following the movement. So it is one tiny step forward at a time, a little more balance, making it easier to relax and be supple which, in turn, will make it easier to be more balanced – so, little by little, you progress towards that good position. For those who are naturally well co-ordinated and have an affinity with horses the process may be pretty quick. Others may take longer, but a good seat is not only for those with a natural gift – it is achievable by everyone with a little effort.

The area where suppleness is crucial is the lower back, from below the waist down to those seat bones. It is the movement of the spine in this area that enables a rider to give the horse freedom to move his back. It also enables the rider to absorb the lift of those moments of suspension in the trot and canter. Therefore the rider has to learn to let go in this area, moving with the horse whilst keeping the spine and head upright, stretched and relatively still.

An exercise to help make you supple — but make sure that you have a quiet pony and that he is held tightly.

WAYS OF LEARNING

There are masses of ways to help develop a good seat, some more effective than others, some easier to put into action than others. You can choose those that are feasible for you, but remember that a selection of ideas helps enormously. Different approaches are invigorating and, by experimenting, you may find one method which helps you to reach the same aim, but more easily, than another. Therefore variety is highly recommended, and it also helps you to become a better and more knowledgeable rider.

WORK ON THE LUNGE

Riding on the lunge is the most effective way of developing a good seat. At the Spanish Riding School, a pupil spends up to a year doing this before being allowed to take control of a horse. The advantages are that a more experienced person has control of the horse, and can keep him going in a rhythm. You can therefore focus on yourself rather than trying to direct the horse, and it will be easier to do exercises. (Work on the lunge can be disadvantageous if the lunger is inexperienced and/or lacks caution; if the horse is wild or disobedient; if you are not in an enclosed area and if you do not have the proper equipment.) So long as you avoid such undesirable circumstances, do as much work as possible on the lunge, perhaps starting with stirrups and reins, then progressing to doing without them first in walk, then in trot and, finally, in canter.

When working on the lunge, the focus should be on the seat bones, stretching of the back and legs, and getting as supple as possible. A good instructor will tell you if bad habits are developing. As you become more competent, exercises can be introduced, so that you learn to remain in balance under more testing circumstances, and become more supple. It will help you to develop confidence if you can perform the following exercises on the lunge: touch one toe then the other; swing your legs back and forth; after lifting your arms up so they are horizonta,l turn to the left and then to the right.

Work on the lunge.

NORMAL RIDING

Whatever horse you are on, you can work to improve your position, but it will be much easier to do this on a schoolmaster type, who has done some dressage and is comfortable to sit on, particularly in the trot. Young horses who might become mischievous, or untrained ones who pull and, are stiff and hard to sit to, will tend to make you more tense and stiff.

Riding without stirrups is the classic way of getting a good seat, but this is only effective if you can relax and are not thrown about by the movement. You can practise this on all horses at walk, and it is a very good idea to start each riding session by spending some time in walk without stirrups. You can use this time to think about the seat bones, and the stretching.

A very useful exercise which you see top riders like Reiner Klimke doing, even in the arena, is to take your legs away from the horse and then let them drop back into place. You will find that this will bring them into the correct position, and you will have released the tension that leads to gripping. Try to get into the habit of taking your legs off the horse's side each time you start riding, and whenever you return to walk.

If your horse is comfortable, then work without stirrups in sitting trot and canter. It will be even better if there is someone watching who can advise and point out any bad habits that are developing.

An exercise which assists your balance and strengthens your legs is to stand in the stirrups when trotting, and not to return to the saddle after each stride. You have to lean forward slightly to keep your balance.

MIRRORS AND VIDEO

Being able to watch yourself in a mirror as you work your horse is a wonderful way of training. You can see for yourself what is good and bad and can make the corrections immediately.

Being able to watch yourself on video after you have worked is almost as effective as watching yourself at the time in mirrors, and the video can capture your work everywhere. Very few schools have mirrors over a large enough area to watch yourself from all angles.

VAULTING

This has long been a very popular activity in continental Europe. It is a relatively cheap way of riding, a wonderful way of giving yourself a feel for the paces, and makes you a better gymnast. It is becoming much more popular in England and, if there is a group in your area, it is an excellent way of helping to develop your dressage.

JUMPING

This is fun, stimulating, and helps develop balance and a feel for the movement of the horse. It is not necessary to jump huge fences, but doing some gridwork, particularly without stirrups, is another good way of becoming a more balanced rider. Start with very small fences, always have a helper on the ground and make sure you get the right distances for your horse's stride.

OTHER FORMS OF RIDING

Racing, galloping across country, endurance riding, gymkhanas and even polo all help a rider to build up a better understanding of the horse's capabilities and to develop balance. With standards in all sports rising so fast, everybody is getting so specialised that many miss out on the all-round early education that is such a good base for dressage.

Key factors
* Attaining a good position that is balanced and supple.
* Balance means weight well positioned to help the horse. When the rider's weight is unevenly distributed, it hinders the horse and can make him lame. Focus on your seat bones being 'glued' to the saddle, positioned centrally and taking equal weight. Stretch back, and head upwards and legs downwards.
* Suppleness helps the horse to move athletically: start by making yourself supple and straight whilst dismounted.
* Learn by watching.
* Learning aids - lungeing on a schoolmaster, work without stirrups, mirrors, video, vaulting, jumping.

CHAPTER 6
COMMUNICATION

BASIC PRINCIPLES

The aids are the language we use to communicate with the horse. As with any language, if we want to be understood we must send simple, clear messages. We have to avoid confusion, so we need to be precise and not talk about too many things at once. In order to make our messages simple and clear we need:

1) A balanced seat. When we are balanced we have control over our hands, legs and seat and can use them to send definite and decisive signals. Equally important, we can stop using them as soon as the message has been understood and the horse reacts.

2) To know what effect is expected from a particular aid.

3) To be consistent in the language used, always applying the same appropriate aid for each specific request.

As the aids are a language, we need to know how the horse will learn that language before we can start teaching it. The horse's mind does not work like a human's. He does not reason and work out what he ought to do: for example because such and such happened he should do this. On the other hand, neither is he a machine, which if given a message, will act in a predictable fashion.

The horse has an excellent memory, which we can put to good use when teaching him. But remember that this can also work against his trainers – if he has had a bad experience he will probably remain very nervous of any similar situation for the rest of his life. For example, if the saddle slips when the rider first gets on a young horse, the horse will be frightened, and only very clever re-training will stop him from always being difficult to mount.

REWARD AND PUNISHMENT

The horse learns through trial and error and we use reward and punishment to show him what we want. The reward may simply be a release of the aid we used to ask him to do something, or perhaps it is the soothing use of the voice, a pat and, just occasionally, a lump of sugar. It is amazing how well horses react to rewards; that pat or 'good boy' produces an obvious relaxation, a flick of the ear, in most horses. Thus rewards are a wonderful tool for us riders to get our message across.

With trust and respect being so crucial in dressage, we do not want punishment to be anything painful or frightening. It should be merely a repeat of the request and, if this is not effective, stronger aids. However, if you are sure that the horse has understood your aids and is wilfully disobeying you, then he does need a reprimand. Your options are a loud growl; a big kick reinforced with the whip to make him shoot forward if he is being lazy; a sharp rein-in to halt if he is running off. As soon as he reacts positively then that crucial reward is needed.

Use of rewards is of most help in building up the partnership that riders seek. In dressage our aim is a horse who tries for us, is eager to do what we want – not one who obeys dourly and subserviently.

MAKING IT EASY FOR THE HORSE TO OBEY

Since we want to help the horse to respond instantly, we must put him in a position from which it is easy to obey the aids. Dressage is not just about training on cue so that when you put your leg back, the horse canters. We must make it easy for him to obey and manage to canter on. When he is balanced, in the right bend, working in a rounded outline and with plenty of impulsion, it will be easy for him to obey your aid. If he has his head in the air and his hind legs way out behind him, it will be very difficult for him to change pace, and even harder to get onto the correct leg.

It is a crucially important and all-too-often neglected principle that the rider must not just apply the aids, but must prepare the horse so that he is in a position from which it is easy to obey them. If you give him the best possible opportunities to obey, the horse will enjoy his work and will be much keener to be trained by you. If he has to put tremendous effort into doing what he thinks you are asking for, he will soon become reluctant and sluggish.

When getting a horse to understand – to learn what you want from him – it helps to put yourself in his place. Try to think like a horse and be aware that he has to work out what you want of him when you increase the rein contact, apply your legs or shift your weight in the saddle. He will not know what these signals mean until you have taught him with understanding, clarity and repetition.

THE AIDS

The most important aids are the rein, leg and weight aids.

THE REIN AIDS

The hands should be held with the thumbs uppermost as if holding large mugs. The fingers should be closed on the reins, and the wrists should be supple and neither hollowed nor turned in. The height of the hands is determined by the aim of maintaining a straight line from the elbow through the wrist to the bit, but it should be compatible with this aim that the hands are close to the withers.

The most basic perception of the rein aid is that when we pull, the horse stops, but although important when first teaching him or when he gets out of control, pulling on the reins has serious detrimental effects. The horse will tend to resist the pull because it hurts him. He will also find it more difficult to step under with his hind legs and this, as we shall see, is central to all dressage training.

The other basic perception of the rein aid is that, when you pull on one rein only, the horse will go in that direction. Again, this is of use in the first stages of teaching a horse, but is damaging in the long term. The pull makes it more difficult for him to step forward with the hind leg on that side. Often, too, all that will happen is that he will bend his neck but will still go straight on. To go round a corner correctly we have to think of bringing the horse's shoulders around, and we need to co-ordinate the aids to achieve this.

Pulling on both reins directs the force backwards, making it much more difficult for the hind legs to step under the horse's body, as is the aim.

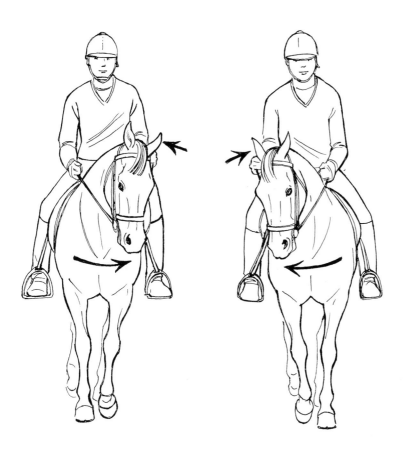

Attempting to get the horse 'on the bit' by a see-sawing action on alternate reins. The horse's head may well come down, but it is usually moving from side to side and it will be difficult for the hind legs to step forward.

Another damaging way in which the reins are sometimes used is to get the horse 'on the bit' by a see-sawing action on alternate reins. The horse's head may well come down, but it is usually moving from side to side; there is no encouragement for the hind legs to step far forward, and that all-important power will dissipate rearwards.

The ways to use the reins are:

Non-allowing: the fingers close tightly on the reins so they cannot slip through, and the hands and arms are fixed so the horse is unable to pull them forward. This is the slowing down aid. If the non-allowing effect does not work, then a momentary hitch can be used. In both cases take care to yield as soon as possible (see Yielding below).

Supportive: keep a steady, elastic contact. This is the normal use, giving the horse a contact he can work towards, but not so strong that he leans and depends on it.

Softening: vibrations are sent down the rein by squeezing with the fingers (by alternating pressure with the fingers as when typing) and occasionally (for a stronger effect) by momentarily turning the wrist inwards. This softening effect is used for turning, to ask for a flexion to one side, and to help combat resistance.

Yielding: the hand goes forward to allow the horse more freedom. Usually the aim is to maintain a contact with the mouth, but occasionally the contact can be released so there is a loop in the reins. This is a reward. It is also a test that the horse is not too strong and relying on the reins to keep balanced.

THE LEG AIDS

The legs should hang down by the horse's sides, clinging softly against them. They need to be under the rider's control so they do not squeeze, kick or change pressure unless they are giving an aid. Getting control over the movement of our legs does take time as the seat needs to be balanced, the joints relaxed, and the muscles supple enough for us to absorb the horse's movement without the legs wobbling. The leg muscles also need to be strong enough for us to keep the legs where we want them. Riding without stirrups is usually the best way of developing the strength and mobility to keep those legs where we want them and thus able to give the light, clear aids the horse will understand. Bear in mind that it is hard for him to distinguish an aid from bumps which the rider gives every stride when the legs are not under control. It is no use complaining about your horse not going forward from the leg if you nudge him every stride and expect him not to react, then squeeze him in the same place and expect him to spring forward!

The main ways to use the legs are:

Forward driving: the legs are applied just behind the girth with quick variations in pressure. This will encourage the horse to move forward and to build up power and energy.

Supportive: if one leg is applied a little further back but with a constant light pressure it will help to guard the hind quarters and prevent them from swinging out in that direction.

Lateral: again, if one leg is applied a little further back, and with the same variations in pressure as in the forward driving aid, it will encourage the hind quarters to move away from that leg and step forward and sideways.

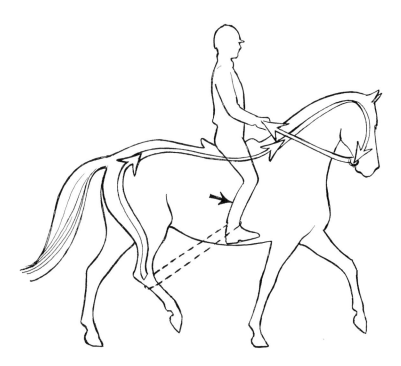

The forward driving leg and, in more advanced training, the seat aid encourage the hind legs to become more active and this energy passes through the horse and the reins to be felt and contained by the hands. The horse is said to be 'connected'.

Lifting the heel to give an aid is a common fault. It usually leads to a loss of position, but this rider is doing well to keep hers upright.

43

THE SEAT AIDS

When you are first starting dressage, the leg and rein aids will give you quite good control over the horse. As you become more effective with these, as your position improves and the training advances, then the seat aids can be introduced. In the highest levels of dressage these are the aids that practically control the horse.

The seat aids are subtle and, as we have seen, dependent on the rider having a good, balanced position. As with the leg aids, involuntary movements of the seat will only serve to confuse the horse. If a rider is unbalanced and constantly rocks or wobbles about, the horse may get used to this and carry on regardless. If, however, the rider then makes a deliberate shift of weight as an aid, how is the horse to understand that this is intended as a positive message, rather than being just another loss of balance, or an attempt to compensate for such? The answer is that he will find it difficult, if not impossible, to make such a distinction.

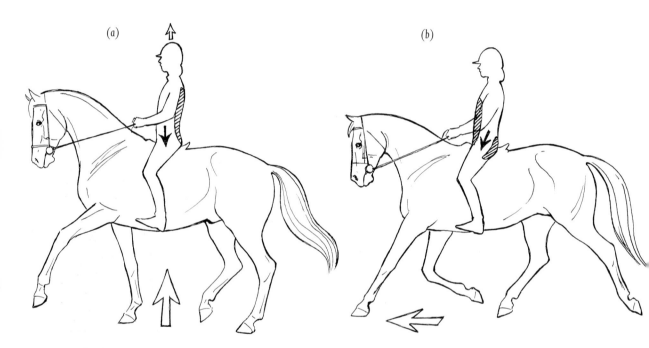

(a) (b)

Use of seat.
(a) Using the seat to produce a collecting effect.
(b) Using the seat to produce a forward driving effect.

The ways to use the seat are:

Putting weight on both seat bones: stretch the body upwards and very slightly backwards and, just for a moment, tighten the muscles in the buttocks and back so that your position is fixed. This will increase the pressure on the two seat bones and encourage the horse's hind legs to become more active and energetic. By using different muscles this can have two effects:

1)   If the muscles tightened are in the back so the emphasis is on becoming taller, then this will have a containing effect, useful in collecting the horse.

2)   If, momentarily, the stomach muscles are tightened and the back is very slightly rounded then this will have that forward driving effect as in the leg aids.

Putting weight on one seat bone: put more weight into the lower leg on one side, taking great care to keep the body upright. (It is a very common fault to lean or collapse a hip when trying to do this, but it results in the weight actually being directed onto the other side.) The result of a correct weight shift to one side is that the horse will tend to move to that side and, as training advances, this becomes the main aid for turning.

Easing the weight on the seat bones: put more weight onto the thighs and the stirrups, while taking care not to lean forwards. This, like the yielding rein aid, is a form of reward and can be useful in getting the horse's back to move more freely.

CO-ORDINATION OF THE AIDS

While it is important to understand how to use each aid independently, in practice they generally have to be used in co-ordinated combinations to be fully effective. For instance, pulling on the reins will probably result in a halt, but the horse is likely to have his head in the air and his hind legs way out behind him. If you want the horse to stay in balance, to keep his power and roundness, then the aids need to be co-ordinated by putting weight onto the two seat bones, supporting with the legs and then applying the non-allowing rein aids.

The upright position just before the transition.

STRENGTH AND TIMING OF THE AIDS

The aim is that the horse will obey very light aids, and this is only possible if he is well taught. The messages need to be simple and clear. If he does not respond to a light aid, the aid can be repeated and, if he is still unresponsive, a stronger aid given. As soon as he obeys, reward him then ask for the same response to a lighter aid. If he responds correctly, reward again. If, however, he is still not listening sufficiently, the process must be repeated until he understands that he must react to a light aid. Note, though, that the aid will be more effective if applied when the horse is in a position to achieve what is asked. More advanced riders will, for example, give a leg aid just before the relevant hind leg is about to leave the ground. This timing is something to aim for.

Applying the leg, seat and hand aids for the downward transition. Note that there is no pulling back.

TWO-WAY COMMUNICATION

Riding is not just about you telling the horse what to do. If you are to become a good rider, you need to listen to what the horse is telling you. It may be that he is stiff on one side; that one hind leg is a little less mobile than the other; that he is sore on one side of his mouth; that his back is a little tight or that he is feeling nervous. It is only if you listen to all these messages from him and try to put them right that you can make him into a willing partner.

The reins and seat are wonderful receivers of messages, so use them to feel what is happening. Make sure that you always include some passive time in your work, when you do not ask anything of the horse, but simply listen to him.

AUXILIARY AIDS

THE VOICE

This is the most wonderful aid and it is very sad (if perhaps more peaceful!) that we cannot use it in the dressage test itself. The horse understands the *tone* of voice rather than the words, so quick, high-pitched commands encourage him to be more energetic, while slow, low-pitched commands soothe him and help slow him down. Using the voice as a back-up means that you need not apply other aids so strongly, and it can help him to understand them. I find the voice particularly helpful in downward transitions: I can use it to get an effect without resorting so much to a stronger rein contact.

THE DRESSAGE WHIP

This is much longer than a normal whip, the reason being not to hit harder but to be able to apply it without having to take your hand off the rein. It is another very useful aid in that light taps with it can reinforce a leg aid, and you can thus avoid the need to kick.

It is important that the horse is not frightened of the whip, but accepts it as an aid which is telling him to use more energy or to step more sideways. Therefore, if he is nervous of it, get him used to it in the stable, carefully stroking him with it and making him realise there is no need for fear.

SPURS

These add refinement to the leg aids, making it possible to give lighter aids – but only if the legs are under control. If your legs wobble about, with spurs on they can bruise the horse's sides. It is therefore wise only to start wearing spurs once you are fairly experienced.

Key factors
* The need to make the language of the aids precise and clear.
* The horse's memory can help or hinder the teaching of the aids.
* The importance of preparation, and thinking like a horse.
* Rein aids: non-allowing, supporting, softening and yielding.
* Leg aids: forward, supporting, lateral.
* Seat aids: weight on both seat bones or just one, lightening seat bones.
* Co-ordinating aids for better results.
* Importance of listening to, not just telling, the horse.
* Auxiliary aids – voice, whip, spurs.

CHAPTER 7
THE FUNDAMENTALS – GO, STOP AND TURN

It would seem obvious that before you can get on with any dressage the horse must go forward, stop and turn when you ask him. Many of you will think you can already do this and will go on to the next chapter, because it is more about the 'real stuff'. However, you may be wrong; many people are. It is amazing how few horses go, stop and turn in a way that helps you to progress. If your horse will do these things correctly, in response to light, simple aids, the rest of the work is so much easier.

The great Finnish rider, Kyra Kyrklund, came to England a while ago to give the annual dressage course. Everybody was agog to see how effective she would be with the horses, some of whom were competing at Grand Prix level. Would she make them piaffe better? This started to look unlikely when she spent most of the first day with these famous horses doing little more than going forward, stopping and turning. She did, however, make all of their movements better, because when she eventually got around to trying them out the horses were more sensitive, relaxed and listening to the rider.

So even if you ride a trained horse; even if you are an experienced rider, it pays to return to the issues discussed in this chapter regularly, and to practise them. They are the fundamentals which make training so much easier. If your horse is lazy, not listening to you or rushing off, it is this stopping and starting that you need to practise. In most cases, the establishment of these fundamentals will provide the answer and there will be no need for some complicated and often expensive remedy.

Dressage can be made much simpler if it is viewed as a series of building blocks, with the basic ones – those that are on the ground – being laid firmly before the next blocks are put in place. Go, stop and turn are the blocks that need to be laid first.

Start the following exercises at the walk and, if possible, in an enclosed area as this will help to keep your horse's attention. When he reacts well at walk, then progress to trot.

HOW TO GO

Whenever you put your legs on near the girth and apply quick variations in pressure, the horse should go forward immediately. If he does not react, repeat the aids and if he still does not, then make them stronger. Give him a sharp kick, and the instant he reacts, pat and praise him. Then try again with light aids. If he does not react, give a stronger aid which can be backed up by the artificial aids – a tap with the whip and/or use of the voice to growl at him. Again, as soon as he responds, give a reward. Your aim is that through being being firm and clear in the short term, you will give him a future when he will need only light, barely perceptible aids.

Precautions:

1) You are just teaching the horse to respond to one aid – the legs, so it is important to

check that you are not holding him back with the reins, which would discourage him from going forwards.

2)   This is the approach for dealing with a horse who *should* know your aids. A young horse who has just been backed will need time to get used to your weight and to understand your aids. He is likely to become frightened and tense if expected to react instantaneously, and he must be given time to develop his strength and understanding.

3)   You can only be justified in giving sharp aids if you are sure that you are not confusing your horse; that you have given clear commands from a balanced, supple position in the saddle.

HOW TO STOP

When you apply the reins — and in this first instance of education it might have to be a light tug or even a quick pull — the horse should stop. When he does so, you can give the reward of releasing the rein pressure, patting and talking to him. If he does not react, it is important not to go on pulling against him. He is stronger than you and is likely to win. Since he must react to a light tug, use a series of them, giving and taking so there is a continual change of rein pressure. The important part is to give the reward as soon as he does stop, because this will encourage him to want to obey you.

Asking the pony to stop.

Rewarding the pony by releasing the reins when he stops.

If the horse does not stop from a light tug, use a stronger one and reinforce it with a voice aid. If he really will *not* stop, head him towards a wall or side of the school and, just as in going forward, give the crucial reward as soon as he stops. Repeat using a light aid (and not into a wall) and, if he does obey, give a big reward. If he does not, continue those stronger aids (and even head into a wall again) until he does.

This is how the message gets through – simple, decisive aids; repetition, reward and punishment. It is amazing how you can turn a sluggish horse into a sensitive one, and an over-active horse into an obedient one through these simple stop/go exercises.

When the horse understands clearly with just one aid what you are asking, then you can start to co-ordinate the aids. This will help him keep in a better balance. We shall think more about this in the following chapters.

Remember, if at any time the horse starts to become lazy, practise again getting him to go forward instantaneously from just your leg aids. If he becomes strong and hurries forward, revert to the stopping exercise.

HOW TO TURN

In the first instance, when you apply one rein by taking it more to the inside (*not backwards towards your tummy*), the horse should start to turn in that direction. However, the problem with using just one aid in the turn is that the horse will usually end up just bending his neck; his body will go straight on and he will find it difficult to turn at all. Therefore, the leg and weight aids are needed to help him bring the rest of his body around.

The aim should be to keep the horse's neck pretty much in front of the withers, the inside rein just asking for a slight flexion so that you can see the inside eye, and the outside rein supporting but allowing enough to achieve this flexion. The inside leg supports and, if energy is lost, drives on the girth, and your outside leg supports further back to stop the quarters falling out.

*A good, balanced turn
(a) on a novice pony.*

(b) on a horse in an internatonal Young Rider test.

You can ride fairly good turns just using the rein and leg aids, so when learning, focus on these first. In due course, correct use of your weight aids will make it much easier for the horse to turn, but these are only effective when you use them from a balanced, upright position. Therefore, start to use the weight aids only when you are confident that you are centred in the saddle. Transfer your weight to the inside by putting more onto your inside knee and foot. This will encourage the horse to turn in that direction. To be effective you need to keep your body erect (think tall); as soon as you lean to the inside the weight will actually tend to shift to the outside.

If you are to stay in balance, you need to keep lined up with the horse. So, as the horse turns his shoulders you will need to turn yours. If you do not, you will find yourself facing straight ahead and balanced for going in that direction when you are asking with your reins, legs and weight for the horse to turn onto another line.

There are two schools of thought as to where you turn your seat bones. The German school says the rider's hips should stay in line with the horse's hips and so, on a turn, the inside seat bone will come forward. On the other hand, The Spanish Riding School keep their seat bones in line with their (and the horse's) shoulders, so the outside seat bone comes forward. You may be interested in experimenting with both methods. For me, the important factor is that you stay centred over the horse, that you stay upright, balanced and with the weight directed more to the inside.

BEND AND FLEXION

It helps to be clear about the difference between bend and flexion. The horse can be flexed without being bent, but be cannot be bent without being flexed.

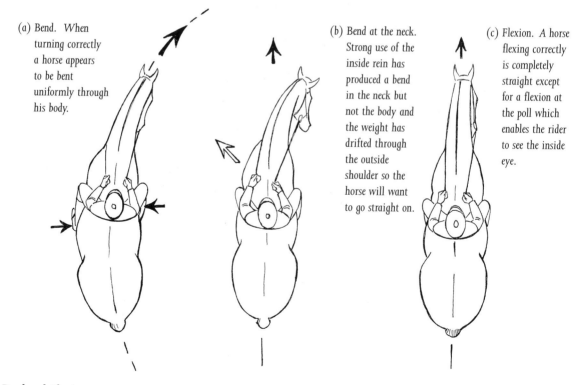

(a) Bend. When turning correctly a horse appears to be bent uniformly through his body.

(b) Bend at the neck. Strong use of the inside rein has produced a bend in the neck but not the body and the weight has drifted through the outside shoulder so the horse will want to go straight on.

(c) Flexion. A horse flexing correctly is completely straight except for a flexion at the poll which enables the rider to see the inside eye.

Bend and Flexion

On a straight line just before a turn, the rider prepares the horse by flexing him to the inside and he will keep the flexion in the turn, when he will also be bent. When the horse flexes, all that happens is that he turns his head sideways around the axis joint – the second of the two vertebrae which join the head and neck in response to an aid from the inside rein. His neck and body stay straight but the turn of the head is enough for the rider to see the horse's inside eye and nostril. This can be seen in the picture of Rembrandt on page 11, where he is flexing to the left. When he does this without tension and resistance the crest and mane flip over onto the inside. If he does it because the rider pulls and holds the inside rein he will 'shorten' his neck and become tense and hard in the hand, and the crest will not flip over. Learning to flex correctly is really important as it helps the horse to be soft and flexible through the poll. This is a crucial and often neglected aspect of learning to work 'on the bit'.

Turning with a very big bend in the neck. This will tend to direct the weight onto the pony's outside shoulder and make it more difficult for him to turn.

When the horse bends correctly he appears to bend evenly through his whole body, and the hind legs follow the forelegs on the track of the turn. The rider should feel as if the horse is bending around his inside leg and not, as is so often the case, around the wither with more bend in the neck than the body. The horse bends as well as flexes when he is on a circle.

Key factors
*   Dressage can be thought of as building a series of blocks, from the bottom up; if the building blocks on the ground are laid firmly, it will all be much easier.
*   The horse must go forward when you use your legs; he must stop when you use the reins.
*   The horse must turn when you use one rein, but better turns are made with co-ordinated rein, leg and weight aids.
*   Flexion is a slight bend at the poll; bend should appear uniform through the whole body.

CHAPTER 8
BASIC GOALS

Many people think of the goals in dressage as being the movements – shoulder-in, piaffe, passage, etc. but, for me, the primary goals are retaining and developing the horse's natural grace and athleticism. It is this good way of going that makes riding so much more exhilarating, and judging and spectating so much more of a pleasure. When the horse works 'with' rather than 'for' the rider, listening to the aids and moving in a balanced, powerful, supple manner, not only will he look and feel good, but he will find all the movements much easier to do.

For the best dressage you should be thinking of developing movement which is more like the loose, powerful action of a tiger than that of a robot, which does what it is told because it has been programmed to do so. Obedience is important, but it need not be obtained at the expense of power and athleticism.

This rider at the Young Riders European Championships is producing the loose, powerful action to the trot which should earn her many marks.

When teaching your horse a particular exercise it may be necessary to forego some of this way of going for a short time while you get your message across. Dressage is a balancing act because there are always so many things you want to achieve. For example, if you want a technically correct shoulder-in, you need the obedience as well as the athleticism, and when you get one you might lose the other. When you are making the horse obedient, and able to turn in a circle and stop where required, check that these aims were achieved without sacrificing a good way of going. If they were partially lost, it is important to work on restoring that way of going before trying the movement again. It is so much more exciting to ride a horse who springs along with free, balanced steps than one who does what you say but has lost his spirit; who is stiff and short-striding.

THE SCALES OF TRAINING

The free, springy way of going can only be achieved if you keep working on the basics. Different people have different ideas as to just what the basics are, but the Germans are the most successful competition dressage riders, and every German rider learns what are called the 'scales of training'. They practise these just as often as a pianist practises the piano scales. The scales of training have been well tested over the years, and are generally accepted as the clearest and most comprehensive way of expressing the basics of dressage.

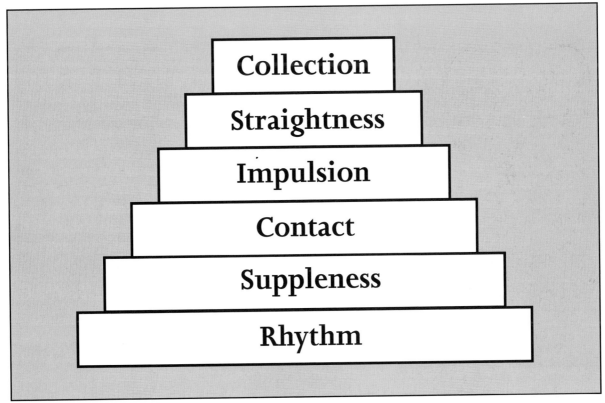

The scales of training.

The scales of training are: rhythm, suppleness, contact, impulsion, straightness, and, eventually, collection. Learn these by heart, and in that order. Although there are times when you skip one point to work on another, you should remain aware of the progression. For example, until the horse works with rhythm, it will be difficult to make him supple; until he is supple, contact will be spasmodic and, until the contact is established, impulsion will be elusive.

Remember, too, that the quality of each and every one of these factors should improve and be of a higher standard as training advances. Therefore, the degree of suppleness accepted in a young, novice horse as being good enough to start working more on contact and impulsion will be much less than that expected of a horse who is advanced enough to learn flying changes.

RHYTHM

Rhythm is important in everything, from playing music to running a race. In dressage, rhythm is crucial. It is also linked closely with another crucial factor – balance. When a horse starts to speed up or slow down the usual reason is loss of balance. When the rhythm is constant the balance is good. There are two aspects of rhythm that need attention in dressage.

1) The rhythm must be correct for the pace – and it changes dramatically between walk, trot and canter.

Walk rhythm is four-time, with all four beats being equally spaced: 1-2-3-4.

Trot rhythm is two - time: 1-2, 1-2, with the legs moving in diagonal pairs. There is a major difference from the walk in that there is a moment of suspension. This means that all the feet are off the ground for a short time; just as one pair is returning to the ground and the other is leaving it. This gives the trotting horse spring to his steps. It is a big fault if he loses this spring and the steps become flat, with no moment of suspension.

Canter rhythm is three-time: 1-2-3, with one diagonal pair of legs moving together. As with trot there is a clear moment of suspension, but canter is different from the trot, not just because it is three-time as opposed to two-time, but because the horse will have a 'leading leg'. He is said to be on the left lead when the left fore (and hind) lands on the ground further ahead than the right fore (and hind). The sequence of footfall would then be: right hind, left hind and right fore together, left (leading) fore, followed by the moment of suspension. The horse will be on the right lead when this sequence is reversed.

2) The second aspect of rhythm is the speed of the rhythm, which is known as tempo. This should be kept constant. If the horse speeds up and then slows down, his tempo is changing and he will be losing his balance. When trying to lengthen the steps in trot, for example, it is very easy to keep the correct two-time rhythm, but not to keep the same tempo. So often, when a horse is asked to lengthen his steps, he loses his balance and starts to go faster.

The aim is to keep a clear, regular tempo, a pronounced, steady rhythm, and one of the skills of dressage riding is to find the tempo in which the horse works best. If the tempo is too fast the horse will become stiff and lose suspension. If it is too slow, the steps will become laboured and he will look as if he is struggling to do his work.

Rhythm goal: correct rhythm for each pace, and a tempo (speed of rhythm) that is regular and suits the horse.

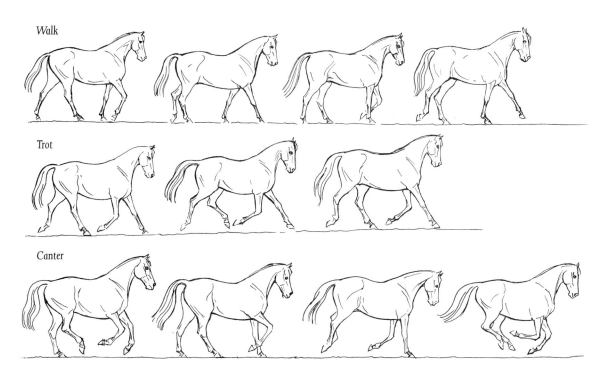

The sequence of steps for the three paces.

SUPPLENESS

Suppleness or 'letting go' is about the closest translation to English of the German phrase *losgelassenheit*. The aim is that the horse lets go any tension in his muscles, his joints are loose and he does not tighten against and resist the rider's aids.

The muscles that are most important are those over his top line from his hind legs over the quarters, loins, in front of the wither and up to the poll. This line is important because, when the muscles, ligaments and joints along it are free from tension and working easily, he will be able to use them all to their best potential and this will help him to move in an athletic, powerful way. When he is using all these parts properly and is not stiffening them we say he works 'through', and his back is 'swinging' (this is shown by his tail moving slightly from side to side). When these top line muscles, ligaments and joints are not working correctly, the horse will tend to be hollow, his steps will be stiff and tight, he will not spring off the ground in trot and canter and he will not be moving athletically. The test of whether he is supple and letting go over his back and neck is that when you ease the rein contact he will want to stretch forward and down and not, as is so often the case, upward.

Suppleness goal: the horse works without resistance; he is loose and letting go.

CONTACT

The contact to aim for is a light, even, elastic feel in both reins. Although it might seem strange, this is achieved by aids from the legs, not the hands. The legs are applied as a driving aid, the horse steps more underneath his body and works through those muscles along his top line which connect the hind quarters and the forehand. Thus the rider feels the energy of a lively forward tendency coming through into the reins. The horse is then said to be 'connected'. His outline and his steps will be 'round', not hollow and flat. He can be ridden forward from behind into a soft contact with the rider's hands.

A young horse working to a good contact. He is connected. It is instructive to note that, although his hind legs are active, there is not the engagement expected from an older horse. Compare with the photo on page 61.

The contact is made because of the forward driving aids of the legs and seat, and the hands are ready to contain this energy. It does not come because the reins are drawn back to take up any slack or to pull the head down. This would only destroy the activity and create resistance.

If you pull back it leads to breaks in the contact just like if you bend your arms when water skiing, or if you pull too hard on the sail when sailing. If, on the other hand, you ride with loose reins, there is nothing for the horse to work towards. A soft, elastic feel with his mouth is what you are after.

Correct contact is a concept that can be hard for beginners to understand until they have experienced it. This is one case where it can be very helpful to ride a schoolmaster; a horse who has been trained to give correct contact.

Contact goal: a soft, elastic contact in the hands achieved by the legs asking the horse to step more actively forward.

IMPULSION

This is the power of the horse. Originating in the hind quarters, it enables the horse to take more energetic steps, to move his hind legs more actively under his body, and it is contained by the rein contact, which prevents him from using this extra energy simply to go faster. Any resistance – tightening of muscles, ligaments and joints – will prevent this energy from getting through, so he must be supple and connected in order to build up real impulsion.

On test sheets, the ingredients of impulsion are defined as:

1) Desire to go forward – the horse must want to go forward, and must not be lazy and unresponsive to your leg aids.
2) Elasticity and suppleness of the back – he must be supple and letting go, so that the energy can get through.
3) Engagement of the hind quarters – this is where the power comes from and, unless he steps forward and under, there will be little energy in evidence.

If, when you apply your legs, the horse steps forward more energetically and allows you to contain the power created with your hands, it is the most wonderful feeling. To achieve this, the horse will need to be working in rhythm and balance, be loose and accepting the contact.

Another of the skills of the dressage rider is producing enough impulsion to maximise the horse's ability and to show off his athleticism, but not so much that it cannot be controlled. If you demand so much energy that the horse starts to pull and you lose that soft, elastic feel in your hands, then you no longer have the ability to control that impulsion. The horse will want to go faster, and will start to resist.

Impulsion goal: to develop and contain the power within your horse so that he moves with elastic, springy steps.

STRAIGHTNESS

Horses, like humans, are born one-sided and will tend to move forward with their bodies slightly curved. This crookedness can get worse if a rider sits to one side and/or keeps a stronger contact on one rein than the other. When a horse is crooked it will be more difficult for him to stay balanced. He will work unevenly, so while he may show reasonably good suppleness, contact and impulsion on one rein, on the other he will be stiffer and find it difficult to keep a rhythm. The feel in the rider's hands will be different, with one side being light and the other rather strong and difficult to soften, flex and bend.

The aim of straightness is that the hind legs step into the tracks of the forelegs both on a straight line and on a circle, and that the rider has an even feel in both reins.

The rider's natural reaction when getting on a one-sided horse is to break down the resistance and to make him bend to the side to which he does not want to turn by pulling on that rein. There is also a tendency to fiddle with the reins to get a more even contact. The problem with this approach is that it tends to damp down impulsion because it is difficult not to pull back on the reins. It is also likely to lead to other resistances as the horse does not like being pulled around. Furthermore, if you have to ride unevenly to keep your horse straight this will lead to other problems. You have to train him so that he will work straight for himself and does not have to be pulled and kicked into doing so.

Concentrate on the hind quarters, where the power comes from. When a horse is not straight he is not taking his hind legs forward towards his forelegs: they will be drifting to one side. If he is ridden positively forward, with the driving and supporting leg aids being used to encourage the hind legs to step directly forward rather than to one side, the horse can be straightened gradually without setting up detrimental side-effects. When you feel your horse go crooked, give him an energetic forward burst (without speeding up if possible) and then settle him back into the original work.

At the same time as using positive forward riding to correct the crookedness, the work on loosening the horse, developing the contact and getting him to take a more positive contact on his light side will help to make his muscles more equal on both sides. As the work advances, shoulder-fore and shoulder-in will give you more control over the positioning of the horse.

The important thing to remember is that, because you are dealing with muscular development, straightening the horse takes time. Therefore, especially with a young horse, be satisfied with gradual improvements and do not become so intent on getting rid of crookedness that you sacrifice rhythm, suppleness, contact and impulsion.

Straightness goal: to get the hind legs stepping directly forward towards the forelegs, so that the horse is straight on straight lines and curved along the line of the circle when turning.

This pony has not straightened as he came out of the corner, but has left his quarters in.

COLLECTION

Dressage makes the horse a better ride: more manoeuvrable, more powerful and easier to control. To achieve this his balance has to be changed; he has to adjust to carry the weight of the rider in the most efficient way. When he is first ridden, he will carry most of this extra weight on his forehand. This is cumbersome: he will tend to run faster when asked to lengthen his strides; he will find it difficult to stop quickly and he will often lean on the rider's hands because he is unbalanced.

This partnership won the Young Riders European Championship. They are showing the collection (engagement, short, active steps and light forehand that would be expected from such a successful pair).

Through training, the necessary muscles are built up and he is taught how to carry more and more weight on his hind quarters. This lightens his forehand and gives him more freedom to move his shoulders, so he will become an easier and more athletic ride.

Over time the horse is asked for more and more collection: his hind legs become more engaged and, as this happens, the weight will be transferred backwards. He will be developing the carrying power of the hind quarters, and they will be slightly lowered. The steps become shorter and higher – not because the rider holds back with the reins, but because the seat and legs are applied to further engage the hind legs under the horse's body. The hands are simply used to prevent the energy from escaping forward.

At Grand Prix level, collection is developed to the extent where the horse can trot on the spot in piaffe or turn around practically on the spot in a canter pirouette. In Pony Club and basic level tests, only work 'towards' collection is asked for when the horse comes into a halt or changes from lengthening his strides to a working trot. In these movements he should step more underneath himself with his hind legs and, as the rider keeps a non-allowing contact, this will lead to the steps shortening.

The goals in dressage are, therefore: rhythm, suppleness, contact, impulsion, straightness and gradually more and more collection. These are needed not just when the horse is trotting around the school, but as the training advances, even when he is in leg-yield, rein-back, shoulder-in and, eventually, piaffe and passage. Whatever you are doing, keep asking yourself: 'Has he got rhythm?' 'Is he loose and supple?' 'Is the contact true?' 'Does he have enough impulsion?' Is he straight?' 'Has he enough collection for what I am doing?' If the answer is 'yes' in each case, then you will be having a good ride and your horse will jump higher, find the cross-country easier and the dressage movements no problem to learn.

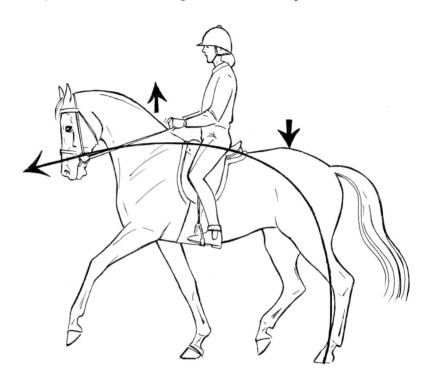

The collecting effect aimed for in downward transitions, and when developing the collected paces. More weight goes onto the quarters, there is more lift up through the shoulders and all of this is generated from behind and not by pulling on the reins.

Key factors
* Aim to keep the basics correct even when attempting a new movement.
* Keeping and developing the basics will give you a much more exciting ride than just asking for obedience.
* The basics are rhythm, suppleness, contact, impulsion, straightness and collection Learn them by heart and keep checking that your horse has them.
* Revert to working on the basics whenever one or more is lost.

CHAPTER 9
MAKING THE PACES MORE BRILLIANT

The paces are a gift from Nature. Watch a foal or young horse running free in the fields – see him hardly touch the ground, he is so light and springy on his feet. This is the brilliance we want to keep when we become his partner, riding him with a saddle and bridle. We have to go through the stages of getting him to adjust to carrying our weight, finding a new balance and learning to respect and obey us. During this time preserving his athleticism is of secondary importance. But when communication and the fundamentals have been established, then we need to think about restoring and developing his natural brilliance.

The easiest way of achieving something is to have a very clear idea of what you want. We can define the goals in words, but it helps to back this up with clear images and sensations of what it is like. Therefore, try to watch riders training and competing on good young horses, and get a very clear picture in your mind of a good walk, trot and canter. If you have a chance to ride a horse with athletic paces, go for it: then try to keep those sensations in your mind and work towards achieving the same ones when you ride your own horse.

THE WALK

This is the pace that tells so much about the horse. If he is purposeful, sweeping across the ground with long, free steps and using all his muscles, then he will usually be courageous and athletic. It is also the pace that is easiest to spoil, as any tension and tightening of the muscles can both shorten the steps and change the rhythm. It is very easy to turn the even four-time beat into an uneven 1, 2-3, 4 and eventually just 1-2. A two-time gait is not a walk; it is called an amble when the legs move in lateral pairs. This is a serious fault, and is usually a result of poor training, which has made the horse tense and unable to use all his muscles. As dressage is about preserving and enhancing the natural paces, the judges will give very low marks for a horse who ambles in a dressage test.

AIMS

Rhythm. We talked about the rhythm in the previous chapter. It is really important for this to be correct in walk, with the four hoofbeats equally spaced, and for the speed (tempo) to help the horse to produce his best walk (if too fast, he will be tense; if too slow, he will be lazy). Watch out for: loss of the correct rhythm, going too fast or too slow.

Suppleness. If the muscles are relaxed he can use them all, especially those over his top line. He can then walk with free, long steps.
Watch out for any tightness or tension turning the walk into a shuffling, short-striding pace.

Purposefulness. The horse should look as if he is going somewhere and wants to get there. He steps towards the bit and does not hold back.

Watch out for: letting the walk become a pace for rest, when the horse slows down and does not really use himself.

An excellent, purposeful extended walk.

A few minutes before the top picture was taken, the same pony had hollowed, and was not working over his top line, so the walk looked pretty awful.

Collected walk. Note the 'V' made by the near fore and hind — this is a good indicator that the sequence is correct and the clear four-beat pace has been maintained when shortening the steps.

A pony with much less training than the grey above shows a willingness to stretch when offered a free rein.

VARIATIONS

Free Walk. The rein contact is released so the horse has the freedom to lower and stretch his head and neck. He should over-track, with the hind feet stepping in front of the hoof prints of the forefeet.

Medium Walk. There is a soft rein contact with the bit, so light that it does not restrict the horse as he walks forward with purposeful, free steps of medium length.

Extended Walk. The rein contact is kept – but only just – as the horse is asked to stretch out and take the longest steps he can without starting to hurry or become tense. This can be thought of as free walk with a slight rein contact.

Collected Walk. The horse is asked to take the shortest steps he can without tensing up, resisting or slowing down. As he shortens his steps by engaging his hind legs more, his head and neck will lift – but not so much that the neck loses its arch. The steps should be active.

POINTS ON TRAINING

Work at walk is a very useful way of training a rider, who does not then have to worry about the unbalancing bumpiness of that moment of suspension in trot and canter. If you are going to do this yourself, it is a good idea to use an older horse who has had some training. With a younger horse, whose muscles are weak and balance unestablished, any rein contact can interfere with the rhythm, cause resistance and lead to a poor walk. When training a young horse it is best to keep to the free walk. Only when he is quite well balanced, and can show the correct basics in trot and canter, should you progress to the medium walk with a very light contact. Aim for the extended and collected walks only when the training is advancing towards Medium level.

THE TROT

This is the pace that sells a dressage horse. A young horse who springs easily off the ground and shows the scope to be able to lengthen his stride will usually be worth plenty of money. Knowledgeable people are aware that good training can improve the trot; that the balance of the pace is what is going to determine whether the horse will do the more advanced work. Huge, eye-catching steps may win many prizes for the novice horse but can be difficult to control, collect and use in the more advanced work. An elastic, light-footed, rhythmical trot is what we should be looking for.

AIMS

Rhythm. A clear, two-time rhythm with a definite moment of suspension is needed. Choosing a suitable tempo is what helps to develop this moment of suspension. If the tempo is too fast, the horse will tense up and will not have time for it; if it is too slow, the horse will become lazy and have difficulty in developing the spring needed to show it. When the tempo is good, the rhythm becomes more pronounced, the moment of suspension clear, and the horse relaxed and using himself.

Watch out for: trotting so fast that the horse scurries along, or so slowly that he is lazy.

A good working trot. Note the active hind legs, but the much more horizontal outline of a novice than that of the grey (below) in the other variations of trot.

A good medium trot with a clear moment of suspension.

Even more lengthening of the steps for the extended trot.

Suppleness. The horse does not resist and can develop elasticity to his steps, using all his muscles, particularly those over his top line.

Watch out for: any tightening of the muscles, especially over the back. The back must be supple, and the horse needs to use his body elastically.

Good hock action. The horse flexes his hocks well and, as his training progresses, he steps forward with them more underneath his body. This will help him to build up impulsion.

Watch out for: resticting the activity of the hind legs by pulling back on the reins, and/or not using the driving aids.

VARIATIONS

Working trot. This is the most natural trot, the one in which it is easiest for the horse to find a balance. The steps are of moderate length; the horse should pretty much track up.

Medium trot. More impulsion is needed than for the working trot, producing slightly longer steps and a little more lengthening of the head and neck, but no change in tempo. The horse should not speed up when he lengthens his steps into medium trot.

Extended trot. This is when the horse lengthens his steps and body to his utmost.

Collected trot. This is when the horse shortens his steps by engaging his hind quarters more, and raises his head and arches his neck. His steps become lighter and more mobile. Again, there should be no change in tempo; it should not slow down.

POINTS ON TRAINING

Training in trot starts with the working pace, progressing to asking for some lengthening of the strides. As the horse becomes more balanced, has more impulsion and stronger muscles, this leads into developing a medium trot and, eventually, extended trot. Similarly, some shortening of the working steps can be asked for – but *without* slowing down – and gradually this can be developed into a collected trot.

THE VALUE OF RISING TROT

Many people feel they are not doing dressage unless they are sitting to the trot. Certainly at the advanced levels, sitting trot gives you much more control, but a major goal in dressage is to maintain and develop the natural athleticism in trot. Crucial to this is that the back is kept supple and the horse works through, otherwise the steps become stiff and flat. Rising trot, (called 'easy trot' in German) is much easier on the horse's back – a better way of getting him to use it, especially if you find it difficult to sit to the trot and are bumping about. It is also important to use rising trot when the horse is young and not strong enough to carry the rider's weight without hollowing against it. It is also a good idea to rise to the trot in the early stages of each work session, when the horse has not been loosened up, and any time when the horse tightens his back during training, as by taking your weight off his back you should encourage him to start using it again.

(a)

(a) *A good balance at the rising trot. The black shadow rider is rising when the diagonal pair of left hind and right fore hit the ground, and the white rider will rise for the other diagonal pair.*
(b) *This is not such a good balance, as the rider is leaning forward all the time. A more common fault is to be upright for the sitting step and forward when rising.*

During rising trot the rider will rise out of the saddle as one of the diagonal pairs of legs lifts off the ground. It is important to change diagonals frequently to avoid any unevenness, and it is usual to be on the outside diagonal – that is, returning to the saddle when the outside foreleg returns to the ground (this can be *seen*) and rising when the inside hind lifts off (this can be *felt*). To change diagonals, simply sit through one bump.

THE CANTER

Like walk, this pace is quite difficult to improve with training, but can be easily spoilt. A powerful, bounding canter is what is sought, but it takes good riding to keep it. So many riders seek a comfortable canter and do not realise that when it gets a bit flat and smooth it will lose that crucial spring and power.

AIMS

Rhythm. The rhythm is three-time with a moment of suspension. As with trot, you need to choose a tempo that will allow this moment of suspension. If the tempo is too slow, suspension will be lost altogether and the canter will turn into a four-time pace; if it is too fast, you will probably be out of control and it will be difficult to keep balance round the corners. Watch out for: holding back with the reins – particularly the inside rein – and producing a four-time canter.

'Uphill'. If the horse canters 'croup high' – with his quarters higher than his shoulders – it will be very difficult for him to stay in balance. The aim is for an 'uphill' canter, with the horse lifting up through the shoulders.
Watch out for: leaning forward and putting your weight onto his shoulders so that the hind quarters lift higher. Keep thinking of riding the hind quarters.

Straightness. It is more difficult to keep the horse straight in the canter than in walk and trot. As he always has one pair of legs leading the other pair, it makes it even easier for the quarters to drift to one side. If the quarters are on one side, impulsion will be lost, as the thrust will go out through the shoulder.
Watch out for: any crookedness on your part which makes it more difficult for the horse to keep straight. Ride him forward positively to help his hind legs move straight.

Correct sequence. The correct sequence for the right lead is: near hind, off hind and near fore together, then off fore. For the left lead it is off hind, near hind and off fore together, then near fore. The canter can become disunited if the horse changes behind but not in front, or in front and not behind. This is very unbalanced and uncomfortable.

Good hock action. As with trot, the hocks should bend well and, as training advances, the hind legs should be able to step further and further under the body. This is the source of energy and impulsion.
Watch out for: pulling back on the reins, which will restrict the action of the hind legs.

Suppleness of the back. As with all paces it is important that the horse works over his top line and uses the muscles which will help him to spring off the ground. If he tightens and stiffens his back the steps will become flatter.

Watch out for: any lack of suppleness on your part. You need to be supple enough to follow the bounding movement of the canter. If your lower back tightens, this will stifle the movement through the horse's back and lead to flatter steps.

Collecting the strides well for this variation of the canter with the shorter steps.

A good medium canter with the head and neck slightly lowered and a clear moment of suspension.

Extended canter, when the horse has to lengthen his steps to the utmost and still keep straight, as this one is doing.

A good 'uphill' canter.

VARIATIONS

These are the same as for trot – working, medium, extended and collected. There is also another form: counter-canter. It will be easier for the horse to turn a corner with his inside leg leading but, as he gets more obedient and balanced, he can be asked to turn with the outside leg leading, and positioned to a slight outside bend. This is a good suppling exercise.

A good balance to the counter-canter, with slight positioning to the leading leg – which is the one to the outside of the arena.

DEVELOPING BRILLIANCE

The key is to keep those general goals foremost – rhythm, suppleness, contact, impulsion, straightness and progressively more collection and, at the same time, being aware of the particular aims of each pace as discussed above.

There are various exercises that can help:

Transitions. All transitions are useful, but those within the pace are particularly helpful for building up the quality of the trot and canter.

Once a balanced working trot has been established, start to ask for transitions from this to a few lengthened strides and back to working trot without changing the tempo. This can be done on straight lines, or on large circles – 20 metres or more in diameter. More and more lengthened strides can be asked for, then medium trot and eventually, extended. Also, transitions can be practised between working trot and some shortened steps, progressing over time more and more towards collection. Try doing this same work in canter.

The aim is to make the horse very supple from head to tail - able to move almost like a concertina - so that he can shorten his stride and outline and then lengthen them fluently without changes in tempo. This will develop impulsion, more suspension and elasticity – all of which will make his trot and canter more brilliant.

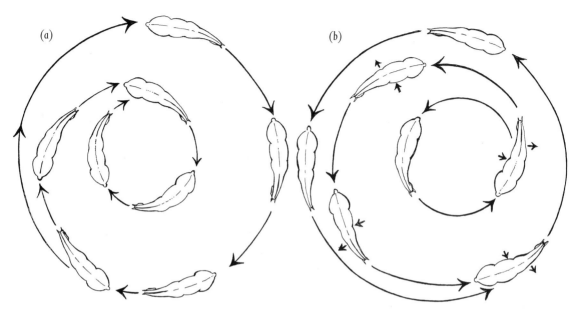

(a) Spiralling inwards from and (b) returning in leg-yield to a 20m circle. This is a wonderful exercise to help get the horse more onto the outside rein and to loosen the back and make him work through.

Work on a 20 metre circle. In trot, spiral in to a smaller circle then leg-yield out, taking care to keep the horse almost straight so he is balanced on the outside not the inside rein. Then, when he is on the track of the 20 metre circle, ask for some lengthened/medium trot.

Work in the open. If your horse is lazy or placid, use the wide open spaces to develop more impulsion. As long as the going is good, use fields or gallop tracks for those transitions between paces, so that he develops more eagerness to go forward. Another horse working alongside can also help.

Work in enclosed areas. If your horse is eager and excitable, work in enclosed schooling areas, try a slower tempo and use plenty of circles and serpentines to relax and supple him in between the transitions.

Key factors
* Develop athleticism of the paces.
* Nurture the natural ability.
* Foster/treasure the correct rhythm.
* Find the tempo that shows off each pace to best advantage.
* Remember that resistance and tightness destroy athleticism.
* Transisitons within paces, developing a concertina effect, building up athleticism.
* Develop the variations to each pace progressively.

CHAPTER 10
TESTING OUT THE BASICS

It is much more healthy to look at the dressage movements as tests of whether you have got the basics right; as ways of improving the basics, than as the goals of dressage. It is satisfying to ride a horse who is obedient and will halt or go into leg-yield as soon as he is asked, but it is so much more exhilarating to ride one who will stay in rhythm, is supple, accepts the contact, has power and is straight – and will maintain these qualities when going into that leg-yield.

In each and every one of the movements discussed in this chapter it is crucial to maintain the basics and it would be tedious to repeat each time that you need rhythm, suppleness, contact, impulsion and straightness. The key is that if you lose them, go back to an easier exercise and re-establish them before trying the movement again. If you do this, your dressage will become much more than an obedience test – you will be developing and controlling your horse's natural ability.

CLEAR GOALS VERSUS HOW TO DO IT

For each of the forthcoming movements I have given an idea of the aids, but remember that it is much more important to keep in mind a clear goal of what you want in the movement, whether it is a transition, shoulder-in, etc. than to keep thinking of how to do it. The particular set of 'how to do it' commands will only work in a certain situation and every time you come into, for example, a shoulder-in different things will happen. Sometimes the horse will stiffen, another time he may slow down, another time barely come off the track, and then next time come off too much! If you have a clear idea of what you want it will be easier to react to correct the fault and get nearer to the goal. If you are focusing on which aids to apply to achieve a shoulder-in and are not thinking about the goal, then the aids are what you will be seeking to achieve, and the actual problems will go uncorrected.

The key to good riding is to know what you want; to be able to feel any difficulties and correct them – ideally before they really develop. To do this you need technical knowledge, but don't let your clear image of your goal be lost in a fog of detail. I love the story in Jostein Gaarder's *Sophie's World* about the tortoise and the centipede. The tortoise was fed up with the wonderful dancing of the centipede and sent her a letter asking how she did it. Did she lift left leg 37 before right leg 38? Or did she lift right leg 17 before left leg 40? The centipede started to think about what she did and how she did it, and never danced again. 'That's the way it goes when imagination gets strangled by reasoned deliberation.'

– so keep those images clear.

TRANSITIONS

THE VALUE

A transition is any change from one pace to another, from one variation of a pace to another and from one movement to another. Transitions are the single most important factor in dressage. This is because:

1) They are such good tests of whether you have established the basics. Any lack of them will result in a poor transition.

2) If the basics are maintained, the transitions are your best means of making the horse more supple, more engaged, more responsive, more established in the contact, and so on.

THE AIM

Even a beginner can make a horse do a transition. It is pretty easy to make a horse go from walk to trot, and this is a transition, but the difficulty lies in trying to get him to do it fluently, smoothly and without losing the contact and impulsion so that he will stay in a rounded outline. Impulsion is relatively easy to keep in an upward transition because you will be using the driving aids to make him trot on or extend his strides. It is in the downward transitions, when the basic instinct is to pull on the reins, that impulsion is so often lost and the hind legs become less engaged. Yet these very downward transitions can be used to increase the activity of the hind legs; to encourage the hind quarters to step under the weight more, so that the horse is more engaged and more collected.

THE AIDS

For all transitions think/feel/visualise the rhythm of the new pace. With a trained horse, this may well be all that is necessary to bring it about.

For downward transitions

In Chapter 7 we mentioned basic transitions made by a simple tug on the reins. This is the way to make the horse understand, but if we are to maintain the basics then we need to co-ordinate the aids. The crucial part of the downward transition is to make the horse engage his hind legs, and to become rounder. We do not want him to hollow and lose power as he would do if the aid was consistently given with the reins alone. Legs and a containing seat (see Chapter 6 and photo on page 46) are applied momentarily. These should encourage engagement of the quarters, and the energy they produce is contained by a non-allowing contact with the reins. This rein contact is momentary, and is followed by a slight yield. Keep re-applying this set of aids until the horse achieves the downward transition.

The voice is a very useful aid when teaching downward transitions. A low, long soothing 'waaalk' or 'trrrot' will help to get the message across without having to use too strong rein aids. Trainer Ian Woodhead gives his pupils a useful concept about the transitions, which is to think in the trot–walk transition of the hind legs trotting for one more stride than the forelegs. This will encourage you to keep your leg aids on to keep him trotting, and this is a crucial part of a good downward transition.

For upward transitions

In Chapter 7 we referred to these being made simply with the legs but, again, co-ordination of the aids is going to help maintain the basics. Moreover, the aids will vary a little according to the type of transition.

If the aim is to lengthen the strides, to obtain medium or extended paces, then the driving aids of the legs and seat are applied. When the increase of impulsion can be felt coming through the horse's back into the hands, the contact can be eased to allow the strides and the outline to lengthen.

If the transition is into a new pace, then the same driving aids are applied with the legs and seat, but the hands should keep the horse soft and not allow him to lengthen his strides and outline. This is because it is a new pace, not lengthening, that is wanted.

Think of the first step of the new pace being taken with the hind legs, because it is they, not the forelegs, that should lead the movements. The horse should work from behind and it is an all-too-common comment on dressage sheets that the horse is not doing so (see Chapter 16). If this new pace is the canter then the aids need to tell the horse which leg to lead on. He is positioned to the inside with a slight flexion (Chapter 7); the weight is brought slightly more onto the inside seat bone; the inside leg is used to encourage activity; the outside rein to stop this resulting in longer steps; the outside leg is brushed back to indicate to the outside hind to start the canter sequence (see Chapter 9).

HITCHES AND SOLUTIONS

Hitch	Solution
Abrupt	Less hand, more leg, think forward.
Hollowing back	More weight in stirrups, lighten seat.
Resistance	More variations to rein contact, keep in a slight flexion. Ask whilst on a circle.
Falling onto forehand (downward transition)	More preparation, establish lighter rein contact before asking, keep your weight back, use more leg in transition.
Losing balance (upward transition)	Build up the impulsion before asking.
Wrong strike-off (to canter)	Need to obtain flexion without pulling on inside rein so try a) on a circle b) by riding a figure-of-eight and asking as you change direction c) leg-yield out on a circle and then ask for canter as you reach the track on a 20 metre circle.

THE HALF-HALT

THE VALUE

This is the most brilliant aid to training the dressage horse as it helps to prepare him for a movement; to warn him that something is about to happen; to make him more balanced; to carry more weight on his hind quarters; to be more engaged and to stop him leaning on the bit and rushing forwards.

THE AIM

The name is misleading, giving the impression of the half-halt being a stopping effect, when the aim is to make the horse more engaged, more rounded and to generate more power. An onlooker should hardly notice that it has happened and it is better to have a series of barely perceptible half-halts than one big one. The result should be a slight shift of weight toward the horse's hind quarters, a slight rounding and lifting of the steps, and a slight lightening of the forehand.

(a) *A half-halt with the rein causes hollowing and the weight to fall onto the shoulders.*

(b) *A half-halt with the legs, seat and restraining hands achieves a more rounding and collecting action.*

THE AIDS

The aids are the same as in the downward transition; legs and seat to engage, hands to restrain, followed by a slight yielding – and that is a half-halt. Remember that the forward aids are the most important as they are the ones that create the engagement. They should be the ones that start the half-halt, the reins being used only to stop their effect from resulting in extra speed rather than more engagement.

A good, pronounced half-halt is very difficult. It is only possible when the horse is supple, taking a good contact and working straight, otherwise it will result in some counter-productive tightening and resistance. Work towards it gradually. Start by asking for only a tiny re-balancing; such a slight collecting action that nobody can see it with the naked eye. It is better to ask for many tiny half-halts than to ask for a bigger one that makes the horse resist.

A good way of developing the half-halt is to start with some trot–walk–trot transitions. Practise these until they are reasonably fluent and the horse stays rounded. Then, from the trot, ask the horse to walk, and before he does so allow him forward. This is the half-halt effect.

THE HALT

THE VALUE

The halt is a good test of whether the horse is listening to the aids, and of the correctness of the transitions. It is also a useful way of developing more engagement.

Pony halting but not engaged; the hind legs are way out behind him, which will make it difficult for him to stay balanced when he moves off.

In this halt the hind legs have come more under the pony. The halt is square, but ideally the pony's nose should be at, or just in front of, the vertical — not behind it.

THE AIM

The horse should not move. His weight should be spread evenly over his four legs so that he is square. He should be relaxed, loose and supple, on a contact and straight. This will all be reasonably easy to achieve so long as he can make a good transition into the halt. (The transition is the really important factor, both into and out of halt.) If the horse can come into the halt fluently and engage his hind legs; if he can move off directly he is asked, taking the first step with a hind leg – and all of this without losing the contact – then he has been well trained.

THE AIDS

These are the same as for the downward transitions, the series of aids being applied until the horse stops. Then it is important to yield the reins slightly (without losing the contact), which will encourage the horse to relax, and not to step backwards.

HITCHES AND SOLUTIONS

Hitch	Solution
Error in transition	See hitches and solutions in transitions.
Horse moves	Use the voice to soothe him, pat him without taking the hands off the reins. If the movement results from disobedience rather than tension, a strong hitch with the reins may make it clearer what you want. Check that you are not applying an aid to move and tapping with your legs.
Forelegs not parallel	Check that rein pressure is equal on both sides and that seat bones are parallel, with equal weight distribution.
Not straight	Check your position and weight distribution. Think shoulder-in positioning before halt, cling with leg on side to which quarters are swinging.
Horse will not stop	Use your voice. Give your aids to halt when heading towards a wall or fence so he has to stop.

SIMPLE CHANGE OF LEG

This is another variation on those invaluable transitions. It is used to change the leading leg in canter. In the first stages of training, and in the easier tests, it can be ridden through two or three steps of trot, but it becomes an even more useful movement when it is through two or three steps of walk. This is because it is more demanding, and therefore a bigger test of whether you can maintain the basics and because, done well, it helps to develop the horse's muscles and his ability to engage.

The key to the training of this movement is progressive development, so that the horse understands what is required. Also, if the degree of difficulty is only increased gradually, he will have time to build up the muscles which will help him to do it with ease.

Start through trot on a figure-of-eight, using very progressive transitions (a few steps of trot before walking, and then some trot before the canter).

The key is to have sufficient engagement and roundness in the canter so that it will be easy for the horse to walk directly. You can use small circles in the canter to help get him more collected, and being on a circle will also help to keep him round when he makes the transition. You can start work on just one rein, making the transition to walk as directly as is possible without too much tightening and, after some clear steps of walk, strike-off on the same leg. If this goes well, try on the other rein. Progress in other sessions to working on a serpentine and eventually across a diagonal. Always be ready to go back a stage or two if anything goes wrong.

The sequence of a simple change.

(a) Good preparation, with obvious collecting of the canter.

(b) Aids applied: rather strong use of the rider's back has led to some hollowing of the pony's. The weight is being thrown onto the shoulders and he is becoming strong in the rider's hands.

(c) *A good recovery as the pony is back in self-carriage and stepping well under his weight.*

(d) Establishing left position for the strike-off.

(e) Rein contact has been lost but the pony is staying round and responding to the aids to strike-off left.

HITCHES AND SOLUTIONS

Hitch	**Solution**
Resistance	This is often caused by the preceding canter being too free for the horse to be able to make that transition. Use more half-halts. Turn him in a small circle before the transition to help collect the canter.
2 or 3 walk steps not clearly shown	In training, walk for much longer and only ask for canter when the horse is relaxed. Then gradually reduce the number of walk steps.
Walk loses rhythm	This is usually the result of tension. Use progressive transitions at first. When in walk, leg-yield a few steps with flexion in the direction of the new canter. (This is a useful exercise when the horse anticipates and/or strikes off incorrectly.)

CIRCLES AND SERPENTINES

THE VALUE

These are excellent suppling exercises. They will help achieve *straightness* by developing a bend to the horse's stiff side, if he is made to follow the arc and not allowed to bend too much on his other side. They help the horse to take the outside rein. They can be used to develop collection, because the voltes – which are the smaller circles of 6, 8 and 10 metres – can only be achieved with rhythm, suppleness, contact and impulsion if the horse can take shorter steps, engaging his hind legs and stepping more under his weight. Thus small circles are a good way of working towards collection. Also, when on the turn, it is easier to ride forward into the shorter steps and to avoid pulling back on the reins – as riders tend to do on a straight line.

THE AIM

To use these figures to show off your horse's ability and prove how well he has been trained. Working on an arc makes it easier to keep the horse soft, in a round outline and working through, so use them not just to show that you can turn, but that the horse can demonstrate correct bend along the arc of the circle, that he can keep his impulsion on the turn, and can show a pronounced rhythm with a good swing in trot and uphill, springy steps in canter.

THE AIDS

Because a circle is a continuous turn, and a serpentine is a series of turns in alternate directions, the aids for these figures are as for turns (see Chapter 7).

HITCHES AND SOLUTIONS

Hitch	Solution
More bend in neck than body	This, like so many of the problems on a circle, is usually caused by too strong an inside rein. Learn to vibrate the inside rein; to limit the neck bend by taking more control with the outside rein. Focus on positioning the horse's shoulders by using both reins, your inside and outside leg, and your weight. Forget about positioning his head.
Quarters drifting out	Check that your weight is to the inside. Support more with your outside leg.
Quarters drifting in	Flex to the outside for a few strides to bring the shoulders in front of the quarters. Think shoulder-in to the inside.
Slowing down	Check that the inside rein contact is not so strong that it is stifling forward movement. Use more outside rein, less inside rein and more inside leg. Prepare better before the turn so that you do not have to rely on the inside rein to pull him onto the circle.
Not a true circle	Ride as a diamond, looking for the next point before you have reached the previous point.

REIN-BACK

THE VALUE

The rein-back is a great way of encouraging engagement, and is a good test of how well the horse is accepting your aids.

THE AIM

Rein-back is a terrible name for the movement as it immediately creates a picture of pulling on the reins to get the horse to step backwards. Certainly, this is a way of getting a horse to move backwards, but he will tend to stick his head in the air, resist the rein aids and hollow his back. All those basics of rhythm, suppleness, contact, impulsion and straightness will be in jeopardy. The Germans – the maestros at dressage – have a much better term '*das Ruckwartsrichsten*' which means 'a forward moving impulse is let out backward'.

This is just what should happen. The rider applies leg aids and restrains the horse from going forward with the reins, so that the best option becomes to reverse. This can be a little difficult for the horse to understand at first, so it is important to teach him progressively in simple, small stages. Always make it very clear what you want, and make it very easy for him so that he never gets confused and starts to become tense.

THE AIDS

Start by teaching the movement from the ground. Tap your horse on his chest, gently pushing him back, and use the voice aid 'baaacck'. Progress to riding, but with an assistant on the ground still pushing the horse back and using the voice when you apply the aids. Then ask for the movement without the assistant but still using the voice yourself. Finally, rely on just the classical aids (see below) but do not hesitate to take a step back along this progressive ladder of training if the horse becomes worried. The rein-back is easy if you keep your horse's confidence, make it very clear to him what is wanted and then give rewards with the voice (and sometimes tit-bits) as soon as he does what you want.

The aids for riding the movement are as follows. Lighten your seat without leaning forward (take more weight onto the thighs), apply your legs quite far back, so the horse understands that this is a different aid from the aid for going forward. Restrain with the reins so that he cannot step forwards. Note that, although the restraining might require a strong contact it must not be a pull backwards. Encourage a soft contact by playing with the fingers and varying the rein pressure. Use your voice: 'baaacck' until he is clear what you want.

HITCHES AND SOLUTIONS

Hitch	Solution
Resistance	This may occur because the horse has halted with hind legs out behind him and lost his roundness, so the movement is difficult to do. Get a good halt before even asking for the rein-back. Keep a soft contact with plenty of finger action.
Hollowing	Often caused by the rider pulling back, so put your elbows in your sides before giving the aids, to make this impossible. Your weight should be light in the saddle, so put more of it onto your thighs.
Rushing	Soothe with the voice. Only ask for one or two steps before riding forward and rewarding the horse. Lighten the rein contact as soon as he starts to step backwards.
Crooked	Check that the rein contact is even. Check that one

of your legs is not further back than the other.
Check that your weight is even in both seat bones.
If the horse always goes to one particular side, then
ask for the movement alongside a wall or fence on
that side until he learns to go back straight.

Horse will not move

Go back to first stages. Make the aids very clear
and give plenty of rewards to help build up
confidence and understanding.

Rein-back.

(a) *A pretty good halt, although
ideally the neck could be more arched
and the hind legs more engaged.*

(b) *When the aids have been applied
the pony has responded. The rider has
done well to take her legs back and
apply them as the primary aid, but
there is a tendency to pull back with
the reins, rather than just restraining.
The pony is tightening his muscles a
little.*

(c) The next step is more balanced and submissive.

TURN ON THE FOREHAND

THE VALUE

This movement is hardly ever used in a test, but it is very useful in early training. It helps teach the horse to understand the lateral leg aid to step sideways, and the rider to stay in balance when the horse is turning and taking lateral steps.

THE AIM

From halt, with the horse flexed to one side, the hind quarters turn through 180 degrees around the forehand, away from the direction of the flexion.

THE AIDS

Ask for a slight lateral flexion. Apply your leg a little behind the girth on the same side as the horse is flexed, asking him to step sideways and around with his hind legs. The outside rein is used to stop the horse going forward and the outside leg stays in a supporting role, being used if necessary to stop the horse rushing around.

As with the rein-back it is a good idea to start the teaching from the ground. Apply your fist by vibrating it and gently pushing in the same place where you will use your lateral leg aid. As soon as the horse steps sideways, reward him, and when he understands that pressure in that area means step sideways, try a turn on the forehand mounted. Remember that you cannot do a turn on the forehand alongside a fence or wall, but need to come onto what is known as the second track so that he will have the room to turn.

HITCHES AND SOLUTIONS

Hitch	Solution
Sluggish response to lateral aid	Use little taps with the whip to support your inside leg. Wear a pair of spurs to help make the leg aid

Horse moves forward	clear to him. Check that your position remains upright and your weight evenly distributed so that you are not making it difficult for him.
	Use small checks with the outside rein.
Horse moves back	Check that your rein aids are not too strong.
Weight onto outside shoulder with a big bend in the neck	Use more outside rein. Check that your weight is not falling towards that shoulder.

WALK PIROUETTE

THE VALUE

This movement helps to get the horse more engaged as, unlike the turn on the forehand, it does require some degree of collection. The horse has to take more weight back on his quarters. If it is attempted too early in training, when the horse is still on his forehand, it will only be achievable by using lots of rein aids and this will often spoil the rhythm of the walk. So until your horse has enough collection to do a simple change quite well, it is wise to keep to half-circles in walk rather than attempt an actual walk pirouette.

THE AIM

To make a 180 degree turn, with the forehand moving around the hind quarters and the horse slightly bent in the direction to which he is turning. The four-time rhythm of the walk has to be kept up, so there should be no swivelling around with a hind leg sticking in one place. He should keep a good balance and neither lurch forward nor step backward – all of which is pretty difficult. The rider needs to remain balanced, must know how to co-ordinate the aids and must be able to react very quickly to help the horse when he loses his balance, bend, suppleness, etc.

As with all movements the walk pirouette is developed progressively, starting with half-circles at the walk of about 8 metres. Then, over time, as the horse keeps up the rhythm and maintains the basics, that half-circle can be made smaller and smaller until it becomes a pirouette.

Good positioning for the walk pirouette.

Two pictures showing turning through pirouette right. The horse is bent around the inside leg and the rider is not having to pull on the inside rein. Ideally, the rider's weight should have been more to the inside, as this makes it easier for the horse to turn.

THE AIDS

Shorten the steps of the walk, but not so much that you lose the four-time rhythm. Flex the horse to the inside and then guide him into the turn with your weight on the inside seat bone. Most novices will find they will tend to slip to the outside, so take care to stay upright with your weight down on that inside stirrup. The inside leg should encourage the horse to keep the rhythm and not let him step backwards. The outside leg is active behind the girth to encourage the horse to turn and to prevent the quarters slipping outwards. The outside rein limits the bend and helps prevent the weight from falling onto that outside shoulder.

HITCHES AND SOLUTIONS

Hitch	Solution
Hind leg sticks in one place	Use more inside leg. Check inside rein is not pulling back. Think more forward. Make the pirouette bigger.
Quarters swing out	More support from your outside leg. Lighten the inside rein. Check your weight, think of being one step ahead of your horse, rather than (as often happens) being one step behind and letting your seat slip to the outside.
Hind legs cross over	Think more forward.
Bend is lost	Check your weight distribution. Go back to a bigger pirouette and when bend is established make it smaller again.
Horse steps back	Lighten rein pressure, think more forwards.
Too large	This is acceptable in the early stages and will make it less likely that the crucial walk rhythm is lost.

LEG-YIELDING

THE VALUE

Together with the turn on the forehand, this is the best way to teach the horse to step sideways. It is a good suppling exercise and is particularly effective at making the crucial muscles behind the saddle work. It helps the horse to work into the outside rein. It also helps the rider as it is a good way of getting a feel of an effective outside rein, and of learning to stay in balance when the horse steps sideways.

THE AIM

The horse is almost straight, with a slight flexion at the poll away from the direction he is moving. He steps forwards and sideways, with both his hind and forelegs crossing.

THE AIDS

Ask for a slight flexion. Apply the leg on the same side as the flexion, close to the girth. This is the action that asks the horse to step sideways. The feeling should be that the horse steps sideways towards the outside rein and enough contact is kept in this rein to keep the neck straight. If there is too much bend in the neck the weight will tend to fall onto the outside shoulder and hamper the freedom of movement.

The outside leg supports a little behind the girth, ready to be more active if the quarters start to lead. The rider's position and weight should stay central. In their efforts to push the horse sideways, many riders lose their upright position and let their weight slip to one side and slide across the saddle. This makes it very difficult for the horse to step sideways.

Having made a half-circle to the centre line, start by asking for only a little crossing towards the track. Progressively ask for more crossing as the horse retains the basics in the leg-yield. Another way of leg-yielding is to go across a whole diagonal: after coming around the short side of the arena the horse is flexed to the outside and then asked to move across. Alternatively, turn along the second track and then turn the horse's head to the wall. When this is going well and the horse has no problem in keeping up the basics in leg-yield with his head to the wall, try the following: after the short side, turn off the track of the long side and leg-yield with the quarters to the wall. This is a good preparation for shoulder-in.

It is a good idea to start all these exercises in the walk and then progress to the trot.

The leg-yield, with the pony nearly straight and stepping sideways away from the direction in which he is flexed.

HITCHES AND SOLUTIONS

Hitch	Solution
Too much bend in neck	Ease the contact in the inside rein. Use a series of half-halts with the outside rein
Sluggish response to lateral aid	Check your weight and position. Try in walk to make sure that the horse understands the lateral aid. Leg-yield in rising trot, as this frees the horse's back and helps you to keep an upright position. Use taps with the whip; use a pair of spurs.
Horse loses impulsion	Go more forwards, less sideways. Ease inside rein. As soon as the horse slows down, ride forward briskly before containing him a little and repeating the leg-yield.

SHOULDER-IN

THE VALUE

The shoulder-in can produce no end of benefits, but only if it is done correctly and the basics are maintained. It makes the horse more supple, helps to straighten him, and thinking shoulder-in is of immense value in counter-balancing the common fault of the quarters drifting in. It is also a collecting exercise, encouraging the horse to step more under his weight, and it helps to make the horse more responsive to the aids.

THE AIM

As the name of the movement suggests, the shoulders (not just the neck) are brought in off the track to an angle of about 30 degrees so that the outside shoulder is in front of the inside hind leg. The horse is slightly bent around the rider's inside leg.

When starting dressage, many people find it difficult to see the difference between leg-yielding and shoulder-in. The crucial contrast is the role of the inside hind leg. In the shoulder-in, it steps forward and more under the horse's weight, thereby promoting collection. In leg-yielding, it steps across in the same way as the foreleg, and this has a suppling effect but not a collecting one. It is important that you understand this difference, because many people think they are riding shoulder-in when they are, in fact, leg-yielding. Not only do the two movements have different training effects, also but leg-yielding will not be accepted as a substitute for shoulder-in by a dressage judge.

THE AIDS

To turn the horse's shoulders off the track you need to soften with the inside rein (but this should be the least dominant aid). The most important aids are the inside leg, which helps to establish the bend and keeps up the impulsion, and the outside rein, which guides the shoulders off the track then restrains the horse from going any further and limits the bend in the neck. The rider's weight is positioned onto the inside seat bone. The outside leg, supporting behind the girth, stops the quarters falling out and turning the movement into a leg-yield.

HITCHES AND SOLUTIONS

Hitch	Solution
Falling onto the outside shoulder	Check whether pulling and/or too strong a contact on the inside rein is creating a big bend in the neck. Aim to bring the shoulders rather than the neck off the track. Use more inside leg and outside rein, less inside rein.
Tilting	One ear is lower than the other. The hind legs are not stepping forward evenly. Uneven rein contact or weight distribution can be causes, so check these points. Use more inside leg to encourage activity. In the short term, lifting the hand on the side where the ear is lower can help, but the long-term solution is usually to work on getting both hind legs to be used more equally.

Various exercises in leg-yield.

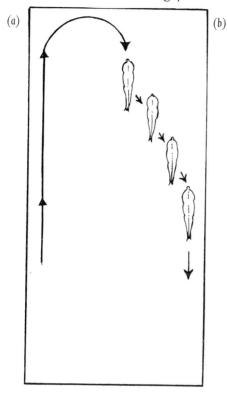

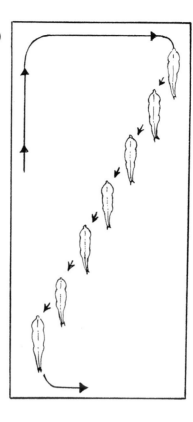

(a) Is one of the best exercises for encouraging the horse to understand leg-yielding. The turn onto the centre line helps to position him to the right.

(b) Is more difficult, as a flexion to the outside has to be established after the corner — but going across the whole diagonal helps the rider to develop good free strides sideways.

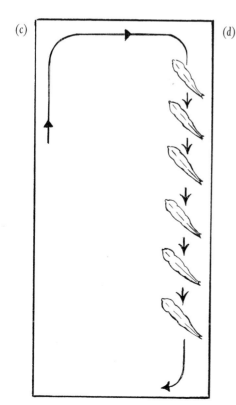

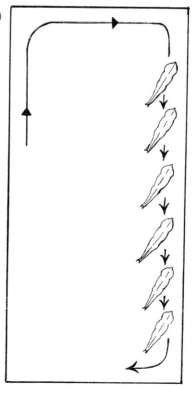

(c) Is useful if the horse is finding it difficult to step sideways, as in this position he cannot go forward to avoid the lateral aids.

Exercise (d) differs from shoulder-in as the horse is at a bigger angle to the track; is straighter, with only a slight flexion at the poll; and is moving on four tracks not three as is usual for shoulder-in.

Quarters out

This turns the shoulder-in into a leg-yield. Give more support from your outside leg, use less inside rein, take the horse's shoulders back closer to the track (if there is too much angle). It is much better to take the shoulders less off the track and have the inside hind stepping forward than to have the hind quarters falling out in a leg-yield.

Slowing down

Many riders are so intent on getting the shoulder-in that they forget about riding the trot, and the horse slows down. Keeping up the rhythm is really important – more legs, less angle.

Resistance

When learning the movement, the horse may tighten his muscles. So long as you keep reverting to simpler work to loosen him up again, this is to be expected. If resistance persists then search for the causes – whether more basic work is needed, whether the horse does not understand (do more leg-yielding), whether there are errors in your weight or rein aids, etc.

Shoulder-in showing good positioning, with a slight bend to the right and the angle such that the right hind leg is stepping almost along the same track as the left foreleg.

(a) *A good shoulder-in for a pony, with active hind legs and clear positioning.*

(b) The shoulder-in of a more advanced horse: there is more collection; the hind legs are stepping more under; the shoulders are lighter; the head and neck are carried higher. (Note that the inside hind leg is stepping forward and under, not sideways as it would in leg-yield.)

HALF-PASS

THE VALUE

It has a terrific suppling effect and encourages engagement.

THE AIM

The horse is bent around the rider's inside leg in the direction to which he is going. The outside legs pass and cross in front of the inside legs. The forehand should be just in front of the hind quarters. When this is achieved with fluency, impulsion and submission it is a wonderful movement to watch and ride.

THE AIDS

Start with a few steps of shoulder-in, then with the weight firmly on the inside seat bone and stirrup, use the outside leg more strongly to ask the horse to step sideways and forwards along a diagonal line. Keep the horse's face placed along that diagonal line as he is asked to step sideways.

Your inside leg is very important as it encourages a bend and keeps up the impulsion.

The inside rein is quite light and is used to soften and guide the horse. The outside rein supports, and controls the amount of bend, the speed, balance, and position of the outside shoulder.

The outside leg asks for the sideways action.

The strength of the aids is varied according to the circumstances. For instance, if the quarters start to lead, lighten the outside leg; if the horse starts to slow down, use more inside leg.

A good way of teaching the half-pass is to turn onto a diagonal in the normal way, and when the horse is balanced, apply the aids for half-pass for a few steps then return to going straight along the diagonal or straight forward. The crucial factor in the training is to make it clear and easy for him, so build up the work progressively, asking for only a few steps before returning to shoulder-in or moving on a straight line.

Remember, too, that it is a very difficult movement in which to stay balanced and upright. In their effort to go sideways, most novice riders push too hard, collapse and slip to the outside – all of which will make it more difficult for the horse to go sideways. Concentrate upon staying upright and taking the odd step sideways as and when it feels good. As soon as balance is lost, return to shoulder-in or a straight line.

HITCHES AND SOLUTIONS

Hitch	Solution
Quarters leading	Lighten aids of outside leg, guide forehand across with outside rein.
Quarters trailing	Strengthen aids of outside leg, check forehand with outside rein. In training, ride straight forwards or into shoulder-in to recover positioning.
Loss of bend	Vary pressure of inside rein, use more inside leg. Go into shoulder-in and recover bend. Check that weight is on inside seat bone.
Loss of impulsion	Use more inside leg. Ride forward straight and

actively before trying half-pass again. Check that
you are not being too strong with the reins.

Head tilting

In the short term, half-halt with rein on side
where ear is lower. In the long term, work to make
the hind legs step more forward more evenly, and
to make rein contact more even.

Good positioning for the half-pass. Both horse and
rider are facing the direction in which they are
heading; the horse's face is along the diagonal line.
The horse is clearly bent around the inside leg, and
the outside leg is further back.

This rider has been over-zealous in his positioning.
There is such a bend in the neck that it is difficult
for the horse to stay balanced, and he is leaning on
the reins to get some support. The rider himself is in
good balance.

CHAPTER 11
INTO THE ARENA

Competing in dressage is a huge challenge. It gives you the opportunity to show off your horse's training, in much more difficult circumstances than at home. It may be easy enough to produce some spectacular lengthened strides in front of your friends when your horse feels right, but it can be much harder to do so inside an arena, maybe on rough going, at a specified marker and in front of judges who are trained to recognise the good and bad points in your work.

LEARNING THE TEST

The first main challenge is learning the test. This consists of a series of movements which cover a whole variety of actions. Study the test sheet, first making sure you understand what is needed, and then start to memorise it. Putting dressage marker letters on the edge of a carpet and then going through the test on your feet helps with both understanding and memorising.

You should bear in mind that remembering where you have to go is just one aspect of test riding. What is much more important is the *way* that you go there – fulfilling the technical requirements and maintaining rhythm, suppleness, contact, impulsion and straightness. The judge will be taking note of these basics in each and every movement, and there are additional marks which relate to them in the collective marks at the bottom of most test sheets. These cover:

Paces – freedom and regularity
Impulsion – desire to move forward, suppleness of the back, elasticity of the steps and engagement of the hind quarters
Submission – attention and confidence, harmony, lightness and ease of movement, acceptance of the bridle and lightness of the forehand.

And it is not just the horse: there is a mark for the rider – the position, seat of the rider and effective use of the aids.

PRACTISING

When you know where you are going and what you want to achieve, it is time to practise with your horse. Try out the movements individually in some form of an arena – preferably one with accurate dimensions. Poles for arena sides, drums for markers and reasonably level ground are all you really need, but generally horses will find it easier to move well and keep balanced on an artificial surface.

Once the individual movements are going well, try running through the entire test – but do not do this too often or your horse will start to anticipate.

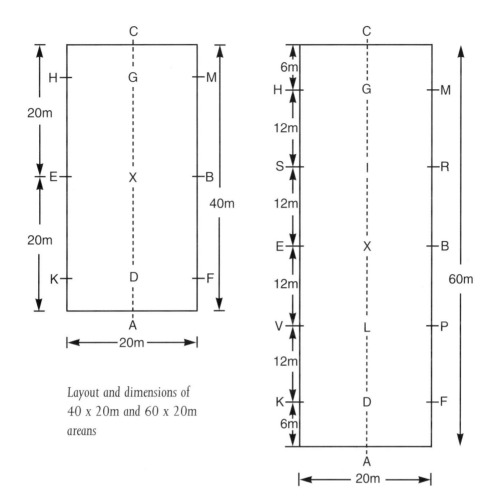

Layout and dimensions of
40 x 20m and 60 x 20m
areans

You can make an arena at home using plastic
drainpipes to mark the sides. It is safer to
put the dressage markers a little further back
than shown.

EQUIPMENT AND PREPARATION

TURN-OUT

The next challenge is to appear in the arena looking good. This does not mean buying the most expensive clothes and tack, but polishing up your existing tack and your boots, cleaning your clothes and turning your horse out so that his coat gleams, his mane is neatly plaited and his tail is pulled and washed.

CHECKING THE RULES

While you are thinking about tack and equipment, it is very important that you check the rules to find out what you and your horse must and must not wear when working-in and during the test itself. The BHS Dressage Group has an official rule book, and the Pony Club and Riding Club movements have similar books of their own. Do check the appropriate book well before the test or you may, for example, find yourself eliminated for not wearing gloves!

PLANNING THE DAY

So many tests are ruined because not enough time was allowed for all that needs doing on the day. It is a very long list, from the feeding, grooming and plaiting, the journey (whether hacking or in a lorry), getting numbers and information from the secretary, tacking-up, putting on your own competition gear, reporting to the steward and then riding-in. Therefore, make a timetable – and allow time for things not working out as planned.

RIDING-IN

This will have a huge influence on the standard of your test. One of the skills of competing is to work out what riding-in programme is best for you and your horse – in terms of both contents and timing.

OPTIONS AND COMPONENTS

The main options and components of riding-in are:
1) Work at home before you leave, or even turn your horse out in the field to get rid of excessive high spirits (but *before* you groom him!).
2) Lead your horse around the showground on a headcollar or, if high-spirited, a cavesson and lunge rein, and allow him to take the odd mouthful of grass. The aim is to familiarise him with the strange surroundings, and with no rider to worry about, he should find it easier to relax.
3) Ride your horse at walk on a fairly free rein (but keep alert and be ready to take more contact if he jumps around). This is a good time to work on your position; to get yourself upright, balanced and stretching the legs. Taking your feet out of the stirrups and trying some exercises can help get rid of any tension, and put you into a better position.
4) Lungeing can be useful in ridding the horse of any high spirits without putting you in danger of being deposited on the floor. Check with the show beforehand that there is room to lunge and that it is allowed.
5) Working the horse deep and low, if he is used to this as part of his training, will help him to relax, stretch and start to use those crucial muscles over his back.

6)   Circles, serpentines, and transitions between and within the paces will progressively build up the basics and improve the degree of collection.

7)   Running through the movements from the test. Remember, however, that riding-in is not the time for making them better than they were at home. The tension of competition means that it will be difficult to get your horse going as well as he did at home, so it is very unlikely that you will be able to improve a movement. Working on a movement over and over again is only likely to build up stresses between you and the horse.

Grazing the horse in hand can help to get him acclimatised to the show atmosphere.

From these options, you can devise a programme according to the nature of your horse and your system of training. Here are some suggestions:

Type of horse	**Possible types of riding-in**
Young	1, 2, 4, 5, 6, 7.
Nervous	2, 3, 5, 6 (and do this work in a slow tempo to help the horse relax), 7. It is important to be able to support him with the legs, and this will be difficult as he will be tending to run away. Do some movements in walk, where it will be easier to insist that he accepts the contact of your legs.
Energetic	1, 4, 5, 6 (again, keep to a slow tempo).
Lazy	6 (a faster tempo, plenty of transitions to get the horse's attention and make him quick to respond to light aids).

Riding-in. Most riders loosen up their horses by working them a little round and deep, with a good arched neck — like this one. Watch that the contact stays light, and that the horse does not fall onto his forehand.

Free-rein work during riding-in, with a chance to check the time.

Riding-in arenas can be pretty busy, so remember to keep to the rules. Pass left shoulder to left shoulder, keep your stick under control and move onto an inside track if you want to walk or halt.

The final preparations.

TIMING

Once the contents of the programme are planned, there is still the timing to settle. Some horses may need just 20 minutes riding-in; others, 2 hours. For nervous, energetic horses who take ages to settle, it is often a good idea to divide the riding-in into several sessions. Do some of the riding-in, then put the horse back in the box or tie him up for a rest before the next session.

Do not forget to allow time after riding-in to take off brushing boots, bandages or anything else that is not allowed in the test, and to give your horse and yourself a final clean up.

RIDING THE TEST

Test riding is a special skill. To improve your overall performance, pay attention to the following key factors:

Showmanship. Learn to enjoy showing off your horse, and the challenge of performing movements to the best of your ability. Nervous riders who put their heads down and zoom around the arena trying to get it over as quickly as possible lose many marks.

Preparation. When watching really good test riders, you can see what they are about to do because they prepare their horses, putting them into a position from which it is easy to carry out a movement. Before a halt you will see the half-halts; before a circle you will see the inside flexion being established and the balancing/warning half-halt being applied before the horse is actually asked to turn.

Reaction in adversity. It is sometimes impossible to avoid a catastrophy. A dog might jump into the arena during your test, your horse might slip and lose his balance, and so on. Remember that such occurrences usually affect just one movement, so write off that movement, reorganise yourself and your horse, and adopt the attitude that the next movement, will be the start of the test. You might get a very low mark for that one movement, but you are in a position to maximise your prospects for the remainder. If you do not reorganise, the tendency will be to rush through the rest of the test, spending your time cursing the dog or that slippery patch of ground, and you will never re-establish a good way of going.

Taking your time. A clear, pronounced rhythm to the work helps earn marks and gives you the time to make use of the arena — to go into the corners, to ride to the markers and to be as accurate as possible without losing the way of going.

The right frame of mind. Aim to get into a state of relaxed concentration so that you can focus on the test, the horse's way of going and nothing else. (More about this in the next chapter.)

Knowing the test. Learn your test really thoroughly. There are so many things to think about, so much that you must do to show off your horse, and you do not want to be worrying about where to go next. If circumstances prevent you from learning the test properly, and if you are allowed to do so under the rules, use a commander. (A commander is someone who calls out the test movement by movement; if it is allowed, you need someone who is good at it.)

Be accurate. If the test sheet says turn left at E, prepare well in advance and turn left at that point. If it says medium trot on the diagonal HXF, then aim to make the medium trot start at H and end at F. But accuracy comes with a proviso. If all you think about is turning left at E and you do not worry if the horse tightens, does not bend, or speeds up, then you will lose more marks because of this than you will have gained for the accuracy. For me, accuracy is the icing on the cake that earns those extra marks when the way of going is well established. Keeping a correct way of going will help to advance your dressage; forsaking it in the interests of accuracy will hinder your progress.

Be specific in your assessments. When you have finished a test, try to avoid passing general remarks like 'He was in such a bad mood today'; 'He would not listen to me'; 'He was really trying'. Instead, focus on things you can do something about. Go through the test, movement by movement. Decide what went well and what went badly. Concentrate on consolidating the good points, and on deciding what work can be done to put right the bad points.

The fascination of dressage competitions lies in the challenge to find ways of getting better and earning more marks. Treat each particular test as the challenge. Look at each movement individually, and work on ways of getting more marks for each one the next time you compete.

The reward for a good test — a championship rosette.

LEARNING FROM THE JUDGE

Judges have been trained to assess the correctness of each movement that you perform. They have to make up their mind in an instant whether it is worth a 0 – not executed, 1 – very bad, 2 – bad, 3 – fairly bad, 4 – insufficient, 5 – sufficient, 6 – satisfactory, 7 – fairly good, 8 – good, 9 – very good or 10 – excellent. They cannot afford a moment's lapse in concentration if they are to do a good job.

Judges work very hard to give you a fair assessment, and their greatest pleasure lies not in telling you how bad you are, but in giving an 8 or 9 when you do a movement really well. Many of their remarks might appear negative, but they have to justify why they could not give you an 8 or 9 and make you realise that they were looking when your horse bucked!

Most judges really enjoy talking about the tests, so if you do not understand what they have written, go and ask what they meant. So long as you do not sound as if you are attacking them, but that you want to learn, you will find them very co-operative.

Key Factors
* Learn your test so well that you can concentrate on important things, like the way of going.
* Work out a timetable for the day.
* Riding-in is crucial. Plan the contents and timing to suit your horse.
* Work out how to earn rather than lose marks in the test itself.

CHAPTER 12
GETTING THE MIND STRAIGHT

Some people are natural showmen; they love competing and are relaxed and focused when in the arena. When they are in front of an audience, and have a judge assessing their performance, they rise to the occasion and produce work as good if not better than they ever do at home. Others are blighted by a lack of confidence in their ability. They worry that they might make fools of themselves; that their horses could let them down; that they have not done enough training; that they might forget their test. Such doubts create tension and make concentration difficult, so that true ability cannot be produced.

It was once thought that confidence and showmanship were natural gifts, which were either present or not, but it is now known that you can train your mind and control your attitude. If you learn to do this, you can beat that dreadful handicap of nerves, tension and lack of focus, and can make much better use of your physical ability.

Through correct mental training, many people have got rid of − or at least drastically reduced − their mark-losing self-doubts. You, too, can re-programme your mind because your mind will believe what you tell it, so long as you are sincere and persistent.

TOOLS OF MENTAL TRAINING
THE POWER OF POSITIVE THINKING

There is no doubt that enthusiasts, people who are quietly confident, have an enormous advantage over those who question their own ability. You have to learn to squeeze those negative thoughts and doubting statements out of your mind and replace them with thoughts that will build up your confidence, for example:

Negative/Doubting Statement	Replacement
That judge hates me.	I am going to show that judge how good we really are.
I always get nervous.	I am going to be relaxed.
I will try to keep my back upright.	I will keep my back upright.
I cannot remember the test.	I will remember the test.
I will not tighten my back in the extension.	I will keep my back supple in in the extension.
I feel sick when I compete.	I enjoy competing.
If I can do a square halt.	When I do a square halt.
My horse is not good enough.	My horse will go as well as he possibly can today.

The keys to positive thinking are: avoid saying out loud anything negative; avoid using 'not', 'try', 'can't', 'if'. Should a negative thought come into your mind, replace it with a positive one.

GOAL-SETTING

Goal-setting gives you an aim, helps you to focus on what is important and helps to develop that all-important concentration. A distinguishing feature of top riders is their ability to focus both on what they are after in the long run, and what they are after at any moment with a particular horse. Top riders are not distracted by outside events: very little will break their concentration on the horse and the movements when they are riding a test.

Goal-setting is based upon four types of goal (see diagram).

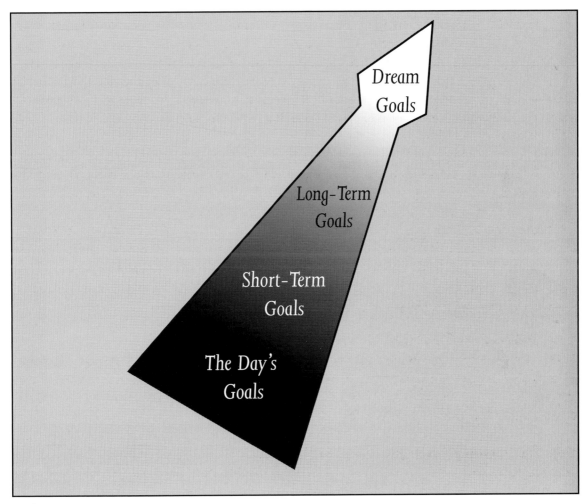

Goal-setting.

Dream goals. The ultimate level, which needs to be set *very* high. Recently, many of the British Under 21 dressage riders set their dream goal as riding for Britain. This may seem a high goal to aim for but, when they achieved it their ambition was drained, and they did not do so well in the European Championships as they did when they were fighting for a place on the British team. If they were to ride well at the Championships, their dream goal should have been a gold medal. Set your sights high!

Long-term goals. These are goals set 3–5 years ahead, which are steps toward your dream goals.

Short-term goals. These are goals achievable during the year ahead, which are relevant to your long-term goals.

The day's goals. These are what you want to get out of a training session, or points for improvement in a particular test.

As you will see, these goals are related, so goal-setting gives you a focus: a path along which you can tread in a positive, ambitious manner.

VISUALISATION

The imagination is a very powerful tool, which you can use to help make your goals more attainable. If you imagine riding well, winning competitions, being a member of a team, being a relaxed, competent rider, this will all help to focus your mind on these things and make achieving them more likely.

Imagination can actually help to improve techniques. For this to be fully effective you need to be relaxed, to close your eyes and to conjure up vivid pictures. If you are visualising riding a horse, think of the colour of his coat, the tack he is wearing, and the feeling his movement is giving you.

Imagining a movement

Use this technique to correct problems by thinking positively. If, for instance, you get crooked in left turns, watch a good rider making a left turn, imagine yourself being that rider, keep the image in mind and bring it up over and over again – when you are in the horsebox travelling to a show (not if you are driving it!); whilst waiting for a bus; before you go to sleep. Keep imagining the detail of riding that corner the right way – it is amazing how much it can improve your technique.

(The important thing is not to imagine the old, bad habits. Banish any negative images and replace them with positive ones.)

Imagining an entire test

It is very valuable to imagine riding a whole test – going through it in detail, movement by movement, stride by stride. Again, the important thing is to imagine the way you *want* it to be, not to think of faults. If you are to maximise your ability, and that of your horse, you need to think of the correct way of doing things.

Imagining a whole test helps you to memorise the movements: to get focused on the test rather than chatting to your friends, worrying about the going or what people will think of your riding; to be ready with the preparations and the aids, and thus to earn more marks.

You can also carry this technique a bit further, and to good effect. Pretend you are a gold medallist like Nicole Uphoff-Becker or Klaus Balkenhol, ride the test like them, treat the competition as they would. Imitating and putting yourself in the shoes of the best riders is a very useful tool.

CONTROLLING THE MIND AT COMPETITIONS

Nervous, sensitive people are likely to have quite a battle with those negative, doubting thoughts that do so much harm to their performance. It might be charming and refreshing to be shy and modest but it is not the route to being a successful competitor. You have to keep filling your mind with positive confidence, boosting thoughts and images. You do not need to be obnoxious and go round telling people that you are the best rider, you are going to win and you are on the way to the Olympics, but you can programme your mind with just these thoughts. You want to have no fear of failure, nor do you want to make allowances in case a problem should arise, because then it will arise. Use positive self-talk to make yourself confident and relaxed.

Use your mental imaging of the test to prepare yourself for the event. Run through it on the day just before you mount and again before you go into the arena to help get yourself focused.

Concentrate upon maximising the marks in the movements you do well. If your horse is not adept at lengthening his strides, but is good at halting and trotting circles, focus on earning the 7s or 8s for these, and do not worry about the lengthening. When I did my first Grand Prix I knew that my horse's piaffe was rather weak, and thought we would be lucky to produce any steps that the judges would think sufficient. I could have worried about what people were going to say about this and spent most of my riding-in time squeezing a little more piaffe out of him. Instead, I focused on what he was good at; where he could earn high marks, and had a 'devil-may-care attitude' towards the piaffe. My highest mark for piaffe was 5 and someone gave us a 3, but I did not mind what onlookers said; I knew the piaffe would get better and that the other marks were good enough to give us a prize. So, do not worry about the problems – concentrate of making the most of what you do well.

DEALING WITH CRITICISM

Criticism is part and parcel of dressage. Do not take informed criticism as a personal insult, a slight on the ability of yourself and your horse. Remember that identifying problems and faults in the training is a necessary part of judging and training. The important point is to see criticism as an opportunity: be grateful that experts have told you about areas that need improving, and meet the challenge of getting on and doing something about them.

Many people, particularly the British, are rather self-conscious about using the mental training described in this chapter. They know that many of the 'old school' will brand them as peculiar. But remember, it is now an accepted part of sports like tennis, athletics and football, and most top international riders use certain mental techniques that suit them. Some may practise these quietly in a horsebox, but others are less self-conscious. Sven Rothenberger, a European Champion, trots around on his feet with his eyes closed and head bowed, going through his test before he gets on his horse.

If you want to earn more marks for your dressage tests, then getting more control over your mind is one way of achieving this.

Key factors
* Think positively and turn negative statements around so they are more positive.
* Set goals for the long and short term.
* Use your imagination to improve your general riding and test performances.
* Treat criticism as something helpful.

CHAPTER 13
THE WAY FORWARD FOR THE AMBITIOUS

Only a few of the many people who take up dressage will have the opportunities and dedication to take the sport very seriously. I did not include talent in this list because, although this and showmanship are needed to become really successful, persistence, ambition and an empathy with the horse are equally – if not more – important. Talented people find things so easy that many of them do not develop the discipline and dedication which are such important parts of dressage.

Those who want to take the sport seriously will need to have a look at the key factors of horsepower, training, and schemes to recognise and assist the talented.

HORSEPOWER

Those who want to compete only in the easier tests can use practically any horse, and so long as the training is good, there is a chance of rosettes. Those who are more ambitious will need to find a horse with correct, athletic paces, capable of earning the higher marks and progressing to the more advanced levels. This does not necessarily mean a horse with extravagant, free paces. Such animals usually cost a great deal of money. They also tend to be more difficult to balance, so although likely to win Novice tests, they often find the collected work of more advanced tests difficult. Therefore, be cautious about being bowled over by eye-catching paces – especially the trot. Most novice buyers are spellbound by the springy, elastic move-ment of a good trot and do not take enough note of the canter and walk. It is much easier to improve the trot than the canter, so it is better to buy a horse with a good canter (clear, active hock action, a clear moment of suspension, elastic steps, good uphill action) than one with a spectacular trot.

The other important feature of a really good dressage horse is temperament. You need spirit, energy and a 'look at me' attitude, and these need to be combined with being trainable – being willing to listen to the rider and take commands without getting too nervous, too rebellious, or likely to switch off and become lazy.

Remember, too, that a dressage horse has to be tough enough to stand up to the rigours of gymnastic training. He needs to be a good, balanced shape and should have passed a veterinary examination.

If such a horse is not bought very young, he is likely to be rather expensive, so anyone ambitious but lacking funds will have to look for a sponsor or an owner who is keen to help a young person. Alternatives are to work in a dressage yard where there are chances to ride good horses, or perhaps to find a difficult but talented horse who few people can ride. In any case, if you need an owner or sponsor, you will have to catch their attention by proving your ability through getting the most out of less talented horses, and by proving your keenness through studying at the yards of top trainers and riders, and being invited onto courses.

In Britain many top riders, such as Carl Hester, Emile Faurie and Joanna Jackson, are not sufficiently well-off to buy their own very good horses. However, they proved their dedication and ability by making the most of opportunities within the Pony Club and Dressage Group schemes, then joined top yards to work for their training and rides.

Another source of finance which can help to provide horsepower is to develop ability as a trainer, and eventually set up a yard where competing can be financed through fees for training horses and riders. The ambitious need be dedicated enough to develop and make the most of such opportunities.

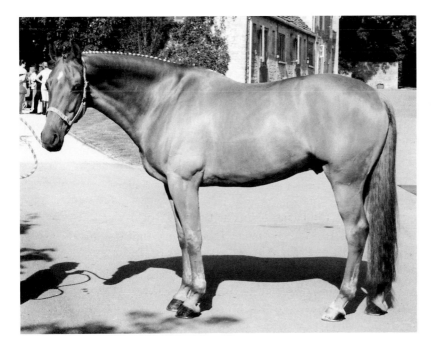

A good dressage type: Enfant, whom Vicky Thompson rode at the Olympics. He was not very expensive as he was small and had an unfashionable pedigree.

This beautiful five-year-old has plenty of talent, but is unlikely to be an easy ride for an inexperienced young person.

RIDER TRAINING

This is a key factor because heading off in the wrong direction can be the end of a promising dressage career. There are many schools of thought, from the High School approach so popular in Portugal and Spain, to the circuses of Switzerland, Russia and Britain, to the obedience-based work of many riding schools. All of these approaches have much to commend them, and people who practise them will gain much fun and satisfaction. But if competitions are to be your aim then you need to find schools whose goals relate to the directives laid down by the international organisation, the FEI. The principals of these schools also need to be in touch with what is happening, and involved in the competition scene as trainers, competitors or judges.

There are different ways of working toward the FEI goals, and this can be confusing if you try out different trainers. The important factor in the early stages of dressage is to study and really understand one system. Riders who work with one trainer for at least two or three years are much better off than those who take a little bit from one and something else from another. Once you have a firm base you can look around to see what others do, and you can decide if this would suit your approach to dressage better.

Because it is best to stick, initially, with one trainer, it is important to make a wise choice of trainer. Look for someone who is good at training competitors and whose attitude and personality suit you as a person. Plenty of research is worthwhile, so find out about the successes of various trainers and their pupils, where the trainer did their own training, and watch the way of going of horses they have trained. Try and find out what people say about the lessons and go and watch some for yourself. It is really important not only that the trainer has a good system, but that you can relate to the way it is put across.

Because the best way of learning dressage is by osmosis – 'catching it' – the more time you can spend with your trainer the better. Weekly or monthly lessons help, but not nearly so much as riding with and watching good people. So if you are at school, choose a stable you can get to easily at weekends and holidays, or even in the evenings. If you have left school you may find that an apprenticeship is the best answer.

In Britain and the USA there is a growing number of big dressage competition yards, and each of these is centred around one of the country's leading trainers. They are excellent places in which to learn, either as a working pupil or by boarding your horse there and spending all your spare time at the yard watching and learning.

A little earlier, we talked about the importance of goals: of having a clear idea of what you want from your horse and your sport. To develop those clear pictures of the way of going you want, take any opportunity you can to go abroad and watch competitions and training. Many countries with long traditions in dressage have training systems which have been operating for many years. An ambitous rider can benefit from spending time as a pupil at one or more of the top schools in Sweden, Denmark, Holland or Germany. Again, before committing yourself, carry out plenty of research into both the quality of the people and the horses they train, and find out what is expected of you. Be prepared for the loneliness of being in a strange country, especially if you do not speak the language, and for the tedium of doing little else initially besides mucking out and cleaning tack. But remember, the Continentals expect you to prove you keenness. They will take note if you seize every opportunity to watch the training, if you look after your horses well, if you are keen to ride anything you are offered. Eventually, most of them will reward you with more and better horses to ride.

TRAINING SCHEMES

Most countries have schemes that seek out young, talented riders and then help them to train. This training is very helpful and so, too, is the recognition which can help in the search for jobs and horses. The German system starts at regional level, with various competitions and courses. In Britain there is a scheme called Talent Spotting, the Under 21s system of competitions and clinics, and regional and central training through the British Young Riders Dressage Scheme.

Finding out about the schemes, and enthusiastic participation in them, is a good way forward for the ambitious. Also, make the most of any opportunities to learn which are on offer: attend clinics with foreign trainers, lecture/demonstrations with your own country's trainers and spectate at top national and international shows where leading riders are in action.

Joanna Jackson, a Talent Spotting Scheme winner who went on to ride for Britain in the 1996 Olympics. This was the same horse on whom, as a teenager, she won the Pony Club Dressage Championships and the National Young Riders Championships. It was Lady Joicey who recognised her talent and gave her the ride.

COMMITMENT

To be a really successful dressage rider requires a pretty much full-time commitment. Only an exceptional person like Dr Reiner Klimke, a lawyer, has managed to combine a non-equestrian career with winning medals. It is difficult to develop the necessary muscle power, technique, suppleness, and fitness without riding three or more horses a day. Most of the serious competitors ride five or six — and some up to fifteen a day. Obviously, the less you ride the more you will need to do weight-training, exercises and work in the gym to get into the right condition. Riding a Grand Prix test requires as much if not more fitness than riding around a three-day event cross-country course.

THE WAY FORWARD FOR YOUR HORSE

The way forward for your horse is the development of more collection. This was touched on in Chapter 8, but I shall now give a little more indication of what is involved, because the ambitious should know what lies beyond Medium level dressage, on the steps toward Grand Prix.

Collection is the last of those goals which we have talked about so often: rhythm, suppleness, contact, impulsion, straightness and collection. It comes last because, in the early stages of training, you can only ask for an active hind leg and an action which pushes the horse forward. It is only as he builds up his strength and balance that he can start to take more weight on his quarters and develop the carrying power which is the basis of collection.

Collection is often referred to as a shortening of the steps (as opposed to their extension), but it is much more than this. If you just think of shortening, this tends to lead to a slowing down; a loss of energy and power. Instead, you should think of a transfer of weight back onto the quarters; a shortening and heightening of the steps so that the horse becomes lighter in front, more mobile and more able to do the difficult movements.

Collection is not an absolute state, but an increasingly high degree of it is required as you go through the levels of the tests. Elementary level tests are the first that ask for a little: the horse will need to carry more weight on his quarters when he changes from medium to collected trot, and before he makes a transition from canter to walk in the simple changes. Progressively, he will be able to take more weight on his quarters and become more able to shorten his steps until he can do piaffe, passage and pirouettes.

As in all work, the key is to retain the quality of the other basics. The collection will be of little value if the rhythm is lost (slowing down rather than shortening), if the suppleness is lost (horse tightens through the back and neck), if the contact is lost (he resists), if the impulsion is lost (the steps become less rather than more powerful), if the straightness is lost (if he goes crooked the energy will be wasted, and he will not be so manoeuvrable).

The work towards collection is largely through transitions: trot to walk, medium and extended trot and canter to the more collected paces, and the simple changes. Shoulder-in is another good collecting exercise.

Collection is obtained by asking the horse to engage more. If the reins are used to pull him back, then it will be merely obedience rather than collection. You need to think of riding *forward* into the collection, so the steps concertina and heighten. The reins are used merely to keep the contact soft and to prevent the horse from taking long steps – they should *not* be pulled back.

Collection will help the horse to become more agile, more maneuvrable, more able to do the advanced movements. These include the flying changes when, instead of having to go through trot or walk to change lead in canter, the horse changes during the moment of suspension. Also, there is the canter pirouette. Although the shape of this movement is similar to the pirouette in walk, being in the faster and more forward pace of canter it is much more difficult, and is only achievable when the horse can collect his canter so much that he is hardly moving forward.

Similarly, in trot, the most advanced movement of piaffe requires the horse to control his forwardness and keep trotting on the same spot. In passage the trot is allowed forward again, but shows such a long moment of suspension that it turns into a dancing pace.

These are the movements the ambitious riders can aim for, but they are difficult and it will take at least two or three years of good training – usually more – to build up the muscles and communication to make them achievable. It must be remembered, too, that this work will require a good rider and a good horse. The easier levels of dressage are within the reach of all, but the most advanced are a tremendous challenge, and many horses simply do not have the physique, mental approach or athleticism to be able to attempt them.

The highest degree of collection is required in a piaffe like this one, when the hind quarters are lowered and carrying much of the weight. In piaffe the horse is trotting on the spot.

Key factors
* Top-class dressage requires dedication and discipline as well as talent.
* The horse needs correct, athletic, rather than extravagant paces, and a trainable but zestful character.
* One system is advisable for the early years.
* Getting abroad to work and or watch is very helpful.
* Collection is the way forward to enable horses to do the advanced movements.

CHAPTER 14
DRESSAGE FOR FUN

The previous chapter gave an indication of what it takes to become a successful dressage rider at the more advanced levels, but there are plenty of opportunities for those who cannot or do not wish to be so serious.

COMPETITIONS

Preliminary level tests can be tackled by any rider and any horse who have had some training. Those who enjoy riding-in with and competing against good riders can do these tests at an affiliated show. For those who prefer more modest rivals, there are plenty of tests run by Riding Clubs, Pony Clubs or equestrian centres.

One of the great things about dressage is that you can compete against yourself. If you are unlikely to come away with a win then there is still the challenge of improving – seeing whether you can do some of the movements, or even the entire test, better each time you compete.

There is also an increasing opportunity to compete in tests that are more fun than the straight ones – the music freestyles. For these, you can plan your own choreography and put together your own tape. These competitions have proved so popular that there is a growing number of variations, including fancy dress and riding the freestyle as a pair or quadrille.

With the sport growing so fast, and an increasing number of people becoming reasonably competent, National Federations are having to take steps to ensure those who do the sport for fun can earn some rewards. America has the Amateur and Under 21s Leagues, and in Britain there are 'A' Rider prizes, amateur scholarships, owner/rider prizes and a host of opportunities for those under 21. There are plenty of rewards within a level even for those who are not that talented, and do not have the time or inclination to improve very much.

The strongest amateur body in Britain is the Riding Club movement, which now finds dressage the most popular equestrian sport. Many small, local clubs run their own shows and competitions under the umbrella of the national headquarters – which is responsible for activities such as National Championships. A special junior membership has been started, and this is proving so popular that there are now many events for youngsters, up to and including National Championships.

The largest movement for youngsters under 21, however, is the Pony Club, which aims to give an overall education in riding and horsemastership. Being a Pony Club member is enormous fun, with activities ranging from camps and dances, to hunting, polo, tetrathlon, eventing and pure dressage. Dressage standards at the Pony Club Championships are becoming pretty high, with international team members often competing, but there are plenty of other competitions at branch and local level which are less daunting for the inexperienced.

TRAINING

Another of the many attractions of dressage is that, while competitions can be stimulating and exciting, everyday training is challenging and fun. Unlike any of the other equestrian sports, dressage has many exponents – some of them top dressage riders – who never compete. They get their pleasure from bringing a horse along, transforming him from a frightened, unbacked creature into one who is more handsome, powerful, and happy to work with the rider to achieve all manner of gymnastic movements.

If training is a wonderful challenge, doing it with other people is more sociable and more fun. Dressage can lead to endless debate as to how to help the horse improve, and whether a particular trainer's methods would help your horse, or produce horses going in a way that would be approved of by the judges. There is much enjoyment and knowledge to be gained from attending clinics – or even watching them – and from working your horse at a centre where many riders do dressage.

In continental Europe, the riding clubs are equestrian centres where riders keep their horses at livery. In the evenings after work the schools will be full of riders training their horses, and the coffee bar or restaurant overlooking the arena will contain supporters and riders who have finished working their own horses. There is great camaraderie between riders who enjoy dressage, and these Continental riding clubs help to promote it. In Britain, more and more clubs of this type are being developed, and they provide an ideal base for those who want to do dressage for fun, as well as for the more serious-minded.

HIGH SCHOOL DRESSAGE

We have talked much about competitive dressage with its directives from the International Federation, the FEI. There is, however, an older form of dressage that the riders and horses of Italy, Spain and Portugal do particularly well. This is High School dressage, where there is less emphasis on the forward-going movements such as extensions, and more on the collected work – the piaffe and passage, and even the airs above the ground. The horses are smaller and rounder in outline, with a high-stepping rather than a swinging, free action, and they can do different things well. High School is a form of dressage which has just as many challenges, but they are slightly different ones. There is much less emphasis on the brilliance of the paces.

Some who do not want to become Olympic dressage riders might consider working with these Iberian horses – the Lusitano and Andalusian breeds – and trying this form of dressage. There are growing opportunities, with Spain and Portugal no longer holding a near-monopoly. Organisations are being set up in France, Germany, Britain and the USA to promote this form of dressage and to provide riding opportunities. There are special competitions which are colourful events, with freestyle and traditional dress being important features.

ROLES FOR THE NON-RIDER

Horseless dressage lovers may find ways of getting rides, and suggestions as to how to achieve this have been discussed earlier. There are also other ways of getting involved in dressage. Many big dressage yards and centres are keen to attract volunteers who will help with every-thing from rolling bandages, to reading out tests, videoing sessions, holding horses at shows and making the coffee. It can be fun to be part of such a big dressage operation.

Volunteers are always being sought to run competitions. Writers are needed to record the judge's comments and marks on each test sheet (which can be an instructive task), runners are needed to collect sheets, scorers to add them up, and so it goes on. Organising a dressage show or even a demonstration requires plenty of helpers. Most of these roles will help you to get more involved in the sport, to learn more about it and to have fun.

High School dressage.

CHAPTER 15
TRAINING PLANS

Systematic training is very important in dressage. Do plenty of research before you select a trainer, but then try to stick with the trainer you have chosen for at least two or three years. Keep to one system until you are confident that you understand it. When you have a real understanding of a system, then you can start looking around and adding to it or varying it and trying to see what is good and bad in others.

The system covered in this book is based on the German one, which concentrates on the development of rhythm, suppleness, contact, impulsion, straightness and, eventually, collection. Within that system it is very important to be flexible and to adjust to the multitude of differences between individual horses. The lazy will need short, sharp work; the nervous, longer more relaxing work; the weak undemanding, quick sessions; the strong can be asked more, and may need a lungeing session to settle. Young horses need to be treated with special sensitivity and given short, varied work, while older horses can progress more rapidly. It is really important to study your horse physically and mentally and decide on a schedule which will best develop your goals.

It is a good idea to keep a diary of how your horse goes each day, so that you will know whether he has made real progress over three or six months, rather than just thinking or hoping that he has.

It is also helpful to decide on your major goal, and the secondary goals you want to achieve along the way (for example, to train your horse for the dressage test at the Pony Club summer show, with secondary goals being two rallies and the Pony Club camp). You then have to set out a plan which will get your horse fit enough for these events, and trained to the required level.

DIFFERENT TYPES OF WORK

Most people think of dressage as something which is performed only in an arena or indoor school, but dressage is about training the horse, and this can be done when out hacking, and jumping. There is much to be said for doing some dressage outside the arena. Most horses thrive on variety to their work, and will be more forward-thinking and willing to obey if the type of training is varied. (Nervous, timid horses are the exceptions to this generalisation as they are happier when kept to a routine.) But even when the type of work is changed, you should still keep aiming for rhythm, suppleness, contact, impulsion and straightness. These aims are still uppermost, whether cantering down a track or approaching a fence.

LUNGEING

This is a great help in dressage training as it enables the rider to see from the ground how the horse is going, the way he trots and canters, and to check on his weaknesses and strengths.

It is a good way to establish communication and get the horse to respect your commands. It helps the horse to develop his rhythm and balance in trot and canter without any interference from a rider's weight and, when he is fresh, it is a good way of allowing him to let off steam without endangering the rider or starting unnecessary battles.

How well all these benefits are achieved depends on how well the horse is lunged. He must wear the right equipment, and attaching a lunge rein to one side of the bit is likely to damage his mouth. The diagram below shows suitable equipment and the way it should be worn.

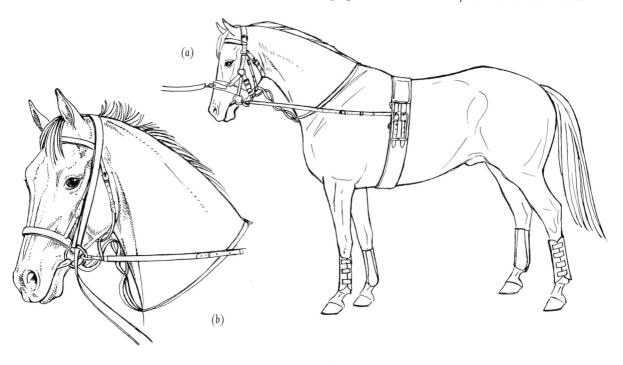

The horse ready for lungeing. It is best to lunge off a cavesson (a) but, for an older horse, the lunge rein can be attached to the outside ring of the bit and run over the poll and through the inside ring as in (b).

If you have no lungeing cavesson, a headcollar can be used.

The aim when lungeing is to establish much the same light, elastic feel through the lunge line as through the reins, and for the lunge whip to be used in a way similar to the seat and legs. The additional, very important aid in lungeing is the voice – low, soothing tones for downward transitions; sharp, shrill tones for upward transitions and to encourage more impulsion.

Ideally, the trainer should pivot around the same point, so that the horse makes a true circle of about 20 metres diameter. The rein and whip should form two sides of a triangle. In practice this is pretty difficult with all but a well-trained horse. Pivoting often has to be forsaken, as it is less important to remain central than to keep in a position to drive the horse forward, and to retain a constant, elastic feel in the rein. To achieve these aims, it is often necessary to move so as to keep level with the girth (or even behind it) and not to end up alongside the horse's head, or in front of him.

It is important for you to learn to lunge under the supervision of an expert, and with a horse who knows the commands. It is all too easy to get in a tangle with the rein and whip and for the horse to take off suddenly with the lunge rein trailing behind him.

Try to lunge in an enclosed arena, and certainly choose a flat area.

Side reins can be attached to give the horse the feel of a rein contact. Start with them very loose and gradually tighten them, but never so much that his head comes behind the vertical in trot. Some trainers do tighten the inside rein one or two holes more than the outside, but it is usually better to keep both the same length.

Lunge the horse equally on both reins. Start with plenty of transitions to ensure that he understands your commands; first walk–halt–walk, then trot–walk–trot. For downward transitions use a low tone of voice, tug with the rein, and move forward so that you are level with or in front of his head. For upward transitions use a sharper tone, position yourself more behind him and, if necessary, tap him with the whip. The canter is much more difficult, so only try when the horse is going with rhythm, looseness and a reasonably consistent contact on the side reins in trot.

POLE WORK

Pole work encourages the horse to be more nimble, to flex his joints and to make more active use of his limbs. Begin with poles on the ground, and once the horse is happy over these they can be put on blocks so that they are 10 or even 15 cm high.

Pole work, the aim of which is to produce good, active steps as shown by the pony in this picture..

It is a very useful warm-up for the horse to walk him over some poles and allow him to stretch down to look at them. The distance between poles will vary for each horse, the important point being to make it easy for him: he should not tense up in the struggle to try and get over awkwardly placed poles. It helps to have someone on the ground to adjust the poles as necessary. For a pony, the poles can be placed about 90 cm apart; for a horse just under 1 m. Start with just one pole on the ground then add one at a time, up to five or six. Then try raising them as described so he really has to lift his feet.

When he finds these exercises in walk easy, try them in trot, using the same progressive training. Start with one pole on the ground and add to them until there are half a dozen; after this raise them onto the blocks. At trot, the distance between poles must be longer, about 1.35 m for a pony and about 1.45 m for a horse.

You can also scatter poles around the field with some at walk distance, others at trot; some on blocks, some on the ground.

As training advances, you can use poles to help with lengthening of strides, by increasing the distance between them so that the horse has to stretch more to step over them. This is useful at both walk and trot.

JUMPING

Jumping has many benefits for the dressage horse. It adds variety to the work and makes the horse more eager, keen and powerful. Gymnastic jumping has the added benefit of being designed to make the horse bascule (round) and use his back. This will help to develop the muscles that are so important in dressage – those over the top line.

Jumping also teaches the rider to go 'with' the horse (to remain in balance ith him) and

Jumping in this style will help to build up those vital muscles over the back, will make the pony more supple, and will give invigorating variety to the work.

122

to allow with the reins in the same way as is necessary when riding deep and low (see Working in the Arena).

Although this book can encourage dressage riders to go jumping and can point out its value, it is beyond its scope to suggest methods and distances. Experts are needed to supervise and advise, especially on distances, which vary according to the horse, the going and the size of the fences. There are plenty of jumping clinics and lessons organised through the Pony Club and individual Riding Clubs, and there also are many books about jumping.

RIDING OUT

Going out in the country is re-vitalising, helps to get the horse fitter, and it is a good place to train. Horses will enjoy their leg-yielding when they do it going from side to side along a grass track. They will be eager to develop medium trots and canters when in a wide open field with good going, and to rein-back when opening gates. Using fields and tracks for some of your training is a good way of keeping the horse thinking 'forward'.

It helps horses to do dressage movements if they have plenty of muscle power and are fit in themselves. So long as the going is good, cantering up hills and along gallops is fun, as well as a helpful way of building up fitness.

A good canter helps to make horses more forward-thinking and fitter.

WORKING IN THE ARENA
RELAXING AND LOOSENING

Start by getting the horse to relax, to work in a clear, pronounced rhythm and to get rid of his tightness and tension. Give him time to get rid of any stiffness caused by standing in his stable or galloping around the field, or of any high spirits if he is feeling fresh and full of the joys of spring.

Riders relax their horses in different ways. Some walk a great deal, first on a free rein, and then ask for some leg-yielding, shoulder-in and, eventually, walk pirouettes. This can be a good method for excitable horses, who are always tending towards rushing and running away.

Others lunge their horses so that they can buck without endangering the rider, and can loosen up free from the weight of the rider.

Nicole Uphoff-Becker loosening up a horse, getting him to work round and stretch over his top line.(NB the Germans might not wear hats in the arena, but you should!)

Others yet work their horses deep and low, asking them to stretch the muscles over their top line (the equine version of touching your toes). The important considerations when asking the horse to work in this way are:

1) The reins are used to soften him, to ask for a little flexion to one side and then the other, but not to pull him down into a shape. These little flexions will help the muscles to stretch and loosen. They should not turn into big hauls, which cause the horse to curve his neck at right angles to his shoulders. Neither should they be asked for in a rhythm, so that the horse develops that mesmerising swing of his head from side to side.

2) He is ridden forward into the contact. Whenever he stiffens against you, or lifts his head, ride him more forward and, at the same time, soften the rein contact.

3) The contact is light and constant, so there is a feeling that the horse is lifting his shoulders and not falling onto his forehand. The stretching must not lead to him pounding onto

his shoulders and leaning on your hands.

4)   You are happy with a little stretching and rounding so long as he keeps a good rhythm, a soft, elastic contact and his forehand is light. (The experts might take their horses *very* deep and low, but the skill to do this takes time to develop and it is easy to it in a way that causes damage.)

It is usually easiest to achieve this stretching when working on a circle or in serpentines at rising trot. Sometimes it useful to canter for a short time, on a circle and in the forward seat so that your weight is not hampering the horse's back muscles.

A test that you have achieved the goal for this relaxation phase is to walk and then go into free walk on a long rein. When you allow with the reins, the horse should stretch more forward and down, which proves that his top line muscles have been made supple. If his head goes up, this shows that his back muscles are sore and stiff, and have not been loosened up.

Remember that, for a young horse, it will take practically all the session in the arena to establish the work so that he is going in a rhythm, is stretching forward and down and accepting a light, elastic contact. As the horse's training advances, these goals should be achieved more and more quickly. Eventually, increasing age will start to make him stiffer and he will again need a longer period of loosening up.

THE WORK PHASE

Once the horse is going in a rhythm, with muscles suppled up and taking a nice contact on the reins, it is time to make him work; to engage his hind quarters more and to develop contained power – the impulsion.

The first stage of this process is usually achieved through those invaluable transitions, starting with trot–walk–trot and gradually introducing some of the endless variety that is available to you. With a horse who tends to rush, who finds it difficult to settle into a rhythm, those trot–walk–trot and trot–canter–trot transitions will be invaluable. With such a horse, concentrate on working on a circle, because on a straight line it will be easier for him to pull forward again. On the other hand, a horse who is lazy needs more work on straight lines to encourage him to think forward, and more sharpening up transitions from trot to halt to trot, and from working to medium paces and back in both trot and canter.

For all horses it is a good idea to combine the transitions with some easy suppling exercises, such as turn on the forehand in the early stages of training; leg-yielding and even half-pass as training advances.

Next, progress to working on whatever basics and whatever movements you have planned for that session, but remember to be flexible. You might have planned a day of fairly advanced work for your horse, but if he comes out feeling resistant or excessively high-spirited, you will need to focus on the basics, and will have to save up the more difficult work for another day.

COOLING OFF

After the work phase it is very important that the horse relaxes. Most riders let their horses do a little stretching again in rising trot and/or free rein walk. This allows the muscles that have been working hard to relax, and ensures that the horse does not go back into his stables or field with them feeling tight. It is also important for him mentally, as the work might have put him under some pressure and he needs to finish with something that is easy.

There are plenty of ways to teach your horse dressage, and many more aspects to it than going round in circles in an enclosed arena. Plenty of variety to the work helps to keep you and your horse fresh. It also helps to get him fit so that he will not tire so quickly and can cope with the more demanding exercises. Plan your dressage training to keep your horse mentally fresh, and to build up physical fitness, as well as to teach him the basics and the movements.

SOME EXAMPLES OF TRAINING PROGRAMMES

Horse at grass, in regular work, one or two feeds a day

Day 1. Lunge 20 minutes, arena work 15 minutes.

Day 2. Arena work 35 minutes, walk 20 minutes.

Day 3. Hack out for an hour and a half, including a good canter.

Day 4. Arena work 35 minutes, walk 20 minutes.

Day 5. Jumping 25 minutes, hack 30 minutes.

Day 6. Pole work 10 minutes, arena work 30 minutes, followed by 30 minute hack.

Day 7. Rest.

Horse at grass. One feed per day.

Day 1. Hack 1 hour.

Day 2. Pole work 15 minutes, arena work 30 minutes.

Day 3. Stays at grass.

Day 4. Arena work 15 minutes, jumping 20 minutes.

Day 5. Arena work 25 minutes.

Day 6. Arena work 15 minutes, hack 45 minutes.

Day 7. Stays at grass.

Horse in stable. Three feeds per day.

Day 1. Lunge 30 minutes, hack 1 hour.

Day 2. Pole work 10 minutes, arena work 40 minutes.

Day 3. Hack out, including work in field, total one and a half hours.

Day 4. Arena work 45 minutes, jumping 20 minutes.

Day 5. Lunge 20 minutes, arena work 45 minutes.

Day 6. Pole work and jumping 30 minutes. Hack 1 hour.

Day 7. Rest.

CHAPTER 16
TROUBLE-SHOOTING

The following are some of the most common problems that dressage judges mention on the test sheets. Note that there are very few universal 'quick fixes' in dressage: generally the cure will depend upon the cause, and causes can include such things as a back or tooth problem in the horse, a shoulder or neck problem in the rider, or a training difficulty in the horse's past. This being the case, there is no practical way of providing a completely comprehensive list of ways to tackle a particular problem. However, the following are suggestions of how to deal with common schooling problems, based on experience.

HORSE HURRYING

Often described as 'sewing machine paces' – the horse moves in short, quick steps. This is associated with tension: when the horse moves in this way it will be difficult for him to let go, use himself, and have time for that moment of suspension in trot and canter.

Try plenty of transitions, especially trot–walk–trot. Avoid riding on straight lines. Instead, work on circles and think of longer, slower steps. Make sure that your weight is back and you are not leaning forward like a jockey, as this puts more weight onto the horse's forehand and encourages him to go faster.

Working long and low (see Tightening the Back) can also help to ease the tension.

HORSE SLUGGISH

There are a numerous possible causes for this and the solution will depend upon the cause. The most likely schooling cause is that he has become de-sensitized to your legs; because your legs keep banging him he no longer responds to them. First, you need to develop more control over your legs. Get them stronger: a good exercise for this is to remain standing up in the stirrups for a minute or so when trotting. The next step is to make the horse much sharper, and to do so, you need to make your aids clear. When you touch him with the leg, make sure he goes forward. If he does not, kick him and reward him if responds; reinforce the aid with the whip if he does not. Remember, to make him light to your forward aid, he must be taught that he has to respond quickly. To achieve this initially you might have to give a very strong aid, but it is better to give one very strong aid than to keep nagging at him every day.

Another common cause of sluggishness is an inside rein that pulls back. A good rider knows clearly the difference between an inside rein that softens by varying the pressure and the angle, and an inside rein that pulls back. Any pulling back stifles impulsion and stops the inside leg from stepping so far forward. The key to good riding is balancing the horse on the outside not the inside rein whenever turning. This is only possible if you are using your inside leg (rather than rein) to ask for the bend, as this gets the horse to step up towards the outside rein and establish a correct uniform bend, rather than just bend his neck in response to a pull on the inside rein.

Of course, the horse could be lazy because he is unwell or too weak to do much arena work, or because he is bored as a result of doing too much. In the latter case, vary the work; go hacking, cantering across the fields and up the hills, and do some jumping.

'AGAINST THE HAND'/STIFFENING/OFF THE BIT

For a novice rider usually the most difficult thing is to get the horse to work round and soft. Everybody wants to get the horse 'on the bit', and becomes so eager to do this that they pull the horse into a shape with their reins. The horse then usually resists, slows down and tries to sticks his head further in the air. It takes time and skill to get a horse working round and soft. He has to be balanced and working in a clear rhythm; he has to be relaxed and letting go; he has to accept a contact – in other words he needs the basics to be established. Work on these and the horse will automatically come onto the bit.

Some older horses might have got used to going around with their noses in the air. Work on the basics will help them also, and for such horses one of the most useful exercises is to ride small circles at walk. When on the turn, it is easier to soften any stiff muscles with flexions, and at walk it is easier for the horse and rider to stay in balance. Ride some very small circles and, when the horse relaxes, keep a positive, balancing contact on the outside rein and ask for trot. Keep on circles (slightly bigger than those at walk), but if he starts to resist, go back to the walk and try small circles again.

When asked to canter this pony has lost his balance and come up against the rider's hands. Holding his head down with strong rein pressure would not help, as he would resist, and this would further reduce the impulsion. Since lack of impulsion was the most likely cause of the problem, work is needed on getting him more engaged and more forward.

'SHORT IN THE NECK'/OVERBENDING

Much the easiest aids to use for steering and stopping are the reins. The problem is that if you pull on them some horses will simply compress their necks or stick their noses closer to their chests. To avoid this you have to ride more from the leg and weight aids.

To turn, transfer your weight to the inside rather than pulling on your inside rein. If you want to collect the horse more, or do a downward transition, use the reins to soften and stop him from going faster but keep your legs on, encouraging him to step under his weight and preventing any shortening of his neck. Your aim is to rely less on the reins, more on your seat and legs; this will allow the horse to carry his neck more forward. Note that this does not happen in a moment. You will have to develop a good position, with clear use of your leg and seat aids if the horse is to rely more on them, less on your hands.

The rein that usually pulls the horse behind the vertical or makes him compress his neck is the inside one on the turns. Nearly every novice rider turns by pulling on the inside rein, and tries to get the bend by pulling on that same rein. The more you can balance your horse on the outside rein, use both reins to turn, and think of positioning the horse's shoulders rather than the head, the less you will have to rely on the inside rein with that dreaded pulling effect. Again, the more you can think of the bend being around your inside leg rather than being in the neck, the more you will lose your reliance on that inside rein.

Sometimes, you will have to ask for a big bend in the neck to break down a stiffness; to help stop the horse leaning on that rein; to encourage him to bend in that direction – but these should be momentary requests, and the important part is then to yield the rein, to be light on the inside rein again.

Remember that stiffness cannot be got rid of in one session. It will take time to make the muscles more supple and loose.

Shortening of the neck can also result from the horse being over-eager and strong, and the rider pulling in an attempt to keep control. In this case plenty of transitions and the same remedies as applied for hurrying should be helpful.

Although his head is in and his neck short, this pony is still working over his top line. If the rider is keeping the head in this position for a short time to help make the pony more supple and submissive this is not a serious fault.

129

This example of a horse short in the neck looks more serious since the neck is not arched and the muscles in front of the wither are not being used. There is practically no contact, so the shortening is a consequence of the horse being contained. Overbending is not very serious if the horse lengthens his neck as soon as the rein pressure is released, but it is far more serious if he does not lengthen when the contact is lightened.

TIGHTENING THE BACK

Dressage people are becoming more and more conscious of the need for the horse to work through the muscles over his back and neck. Whenever these tighten the horse will lose his rounded shape, the steps will come less springy and elastic and he will become less athletic. To get the muscles to work and to keep them working requires constant nursing from the moment the horse is first ridden. His first reaction to the unfamiliar weight of the rider will probably be to tighten his back muscles and hollow them away from it.

To get the muscles working rather than tightening they have to be made strong enough for the horse to move in an arched, rather than hollow, outline. A horse who has little muscular development over the neck and back will need to have the muscles built up through hill work and lungeing. If you do work with experts, you could ask them to lunge him in a chambon at the walk and trot, working the horse in a rounded outline, working him long and low so that he stretches and learns to use the muscles on his top line, keeping your weight off his back by using rising trot and forward seat in canter.

Whenever these neck and back muscles tighten, you must soften and loosen them as soon as possible. The major areas to focus on are:

The poll. The horse needs to be able to flex to either side, just turning his head so that you can see his eye on that side. The neck should stay straight. He should not be allowed to evade this turning and softening action by tilting his head so that one ear is lower. Any tightening in this area makes it very difficult for the horse to work through properly from behind. (See also Head Tilting.)

The muscles in front of the wither where the neck joins on. Often, the neck is lifted and the muscles just beyond the wither crinkle – you will see lines in this area and the neck will not be able to arch. The muscles under the neck will start working and the horse will tend to lose the elasticity to his steps. You will need to lower his neck, and allow him to round and use the muscles in front of the wither. As soon as you feel him tightening, ask him to lower and round his neck so that these muscles work again. It is amazing how often this will reduce the tightening (see photo on page 124).

The muscles behind the saddle. When these are working, the back will tend to round up rather than hollow away from the rider. The steps will become more elastic. Ill-fitting saddles or cumbersome, unbalanced riders can often be reasons for these muscles particular tightening. If neither is the cause, it usually helps to stretch your horse, and the most common way of doing so, is to get him working long and low. Working this way has a similar effect on the horse as touching our toes has on us. When the horse works forward and down the muscles over his top line are stretched and loosened, and any tightening is eased. The main proviso is that he does not fall onto his forehand, so the feeling should be that the shoulders come up with the back, and it is only his neck that lowers.

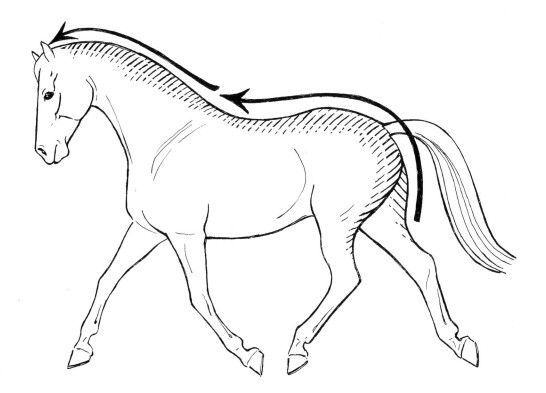

This illustration shows the areas in which it is crucial for the muscles to be supple and strong. Any tightening/resistance or weakness in these areas will inhibit elasticity, spring, and roundness, which are so important for good quality dressage work, and for getting a horse connected and working through.

NOT WORKING FROM BEHIND

This is a common comment from the judges. They see the horse 'taking off' across the diagonal, lengthening his outline but just running onto the forehand. Or they see the horse move off from the halt not directly into trot, but leaning more onto the reins and walking a few steps before pulling off into a rather flat trot.

When the horse works from behind, his first steps into each new movement should start from behind, so that he springs into the pace and does not pull himself flatly forward. The rider has to keep thinking about this power starting from behind. When you want to lengthen the steps, first build up the power behind with your driving aids. Only when you can feel this power coming forward, when there is a thrust from behind that changes the type of contact in the reins, then – and only then – do you ease the contact slightly so that the horse can lengthen his steps and outline. If you ease the contact before the power is created behind, the horse will not be working properly and will tend to run onto his forehand.

The driving aids should start any transition into a faster pace or longer steps, and the horse must be made to respond to these by taking energetic steps with his hind legs before the contact is eased to allow him more forward. Transitions, particularly those trot-walk-trot ones, are the best exercises to help the horse work from behind, and for you to get the feel of the power being generated in the hind quarters.

PROBLEMS WITH LENGTHENING

For the novice, this is often the first serious challenge. Most can manage to walk, trot, canter, turn and stop, but when it gets to lengthening the steps, that is more difficult. The first thing to be very clear about is that it is not the case that a horse will or will not lengthen – if you can give him the right cue he *will* do it. In order to lengthen his steps and keep the tempo he has to be able to generate the power from behind (take active, engaged steps). He needs to have sufficient muscle power in his back and hind quarters to enable him to do so, and he needs to be moving in a way that will allow him to use that power.

First, then, you have to ask whether the horse is strong enough to lengthen his steps. Youngsters are often too weak to do so and will need to be strengthened up by hacking out, work on the lunge and some basic school work. Once this is achieved, you have to get the horse working in a way from which he can be expected to lengthen. If he is stiff in his back, work him long and low for ten minutes or so, then work him up again. Do some leg-yielding, making him really stretch across sideways and use the muscles in his back. If he is not yet engaged enough, it is back to those transitions again – and perhaps some rein-back as well.

The aim is to put the horse in a position where his physique and way of going permit him to lengthen his steps. Before you ask for the lengthening, build up the power. Ask for more activity and engagement, and make sure that he is 'in front of the leg', ready to respond to your aids. If you are going to lengthen across a diagonal, use the short side of the arena to put the horse in a position from which it will be easier for him to lengthen.

Some exercises that help include:
1) Trotting across open fields with another horse who can lengthen. This will encourage yours to try as well.
2) Spiralling into a smaller circle then coming out onto the bigger, 20 metre circle by

leg-yielding. As soon as you hit the outer track, ask your horse to go forward in lengthened strides.

3)   After some counter-canter, make a forward transition into trot and immediately ask for some lengthened strides.

HORSE WILL NOT STAND STILL IN HALT

This annoying habit usually starts because, in the early stages of training, the rider kept on making the horse move a leg in an effort to get him to stand square. It is better to accept that a young horse is unbalanced, and not to worry about halting square initially. Instead, work on getting the horse more balanced and better at the transition into the halt, which will make it much easier for him to halt square.

If horses are worried about being in the right position they will often keep moving when asked to halt. If this has happened, then you will have to get rid of some of the anxiety. Lots of soothing voice aids, plenty of pats and some massage in front of the withers (at that point where horses nibble each other) can help. Spending hours patiently practising halts in the arena and when hacking is the long-term solution to the problem. I sometimes carry sugar and, when the horse halts, lean down and give him some – which is distracting and rewarding.

HORSE WILL NOT BEND ON ONE SIDE

All horses are crooked. Getting them to work forward, to use their hind legs evenly rather than to one side, getting them to turn in circles and serpentines are the basic ways of straightening young horses. If an older horse is stiff on one side, more drastic measures may be needed. Lungeing is useful, and the side rein on the side to which he will not bend can be tightened two or three holes more than the other. Counter-flexion is a wonderful aid; asking for an outside flexion on the side to which he is reluctant to bend. Therefore, if the horse is stiff to the left, ride round the arena on the right rein and ask for a left flexion down the long side, or even for short periods on a 20 metre circle. Most exercises will help loosen up one side: leg-yielding, shoulder-in, loops off the track and serpentines. Remember in all of these exercises that while you are working on softening the stiff side, you should also be asking the horse to take a more positive contact on the light side. When he does this, he will come lighter on his stiff side. Remember too that stiffness is not remedied quickly: it takes time to make the muscles more supple.

HORSE FALLING ONTO OUTSIDE SHOULDER

There are quite a few causes of this common fault. The hind quarters could be drifting in, which will direct weight onto the outside shoulder. Riding more forward, and positioning as for shoulder-in are possible remedies for this. The most common cause of the weight on the outside shoulder, however, is riders mistakenly thinking they are making their horses bend when they are just pulling the neck inwards. This results in the neck bending at the withers, and the weight tending towards the outside shoulder. The long-term aim must be to ask for a bend around your inside leg, not trying to obtain it by pulling on the inside rein. In the short term, counter-flexion can help to position the shoulders to the inside. So, of course, can taking more contact with the outside rein so that the neck is not allowed to bend so far to the inside.

The rider wants to turn right, but the direction of the weight is to the pony's left and through the outside shoulder. The rider is trying to get him right by leaning, but his weight has actually slipped to the outside.

BALANCE LOST

It is not surprising that this term is seen on many test sheets, since balance is so fundamental to dressage (and to many other sports and activities) that most problems can be traced to a loss of it. The most common results of loss of balance are changes in rhythm and the horse lifting his head to help him keep his balance. Balance can be lost because the horse is not straight, because he is not stepping forward evenly with his hind legs, because he has insufficient power for a movement (has lost impulsion), or because he has fallen onto the forehand. Most of dressage is about getting the horse more balanced longitudinally and laterally. The rider, the contact and the use of the horse's hind legs all have to be balanced, but the fundamental re-balancing involves getting more weight onto the hind quarters, and off the forehand. The way this is done is through riding transitions, small circles, and some rein-back. The importance of the rider's position must not be underestimated; the rider's weight must be centred and balanced, and not so far forward that it is encouraging the horse to fall onto his forehand. The horse has little hope of staying balanced if his rider is not balanced on top of him.

ON THE FOREHAND

This is the most frequent reason for loss of balance. It is a loss of longitudinal balance when the horse carries so much weight on his forehand that he will find it difficult to work with rhythm and move his shoulders freely. He will tend to pound into the ground, the steps will run along, and there will be no clear suspension in the trot and canter. He will be destroying his natural athleticism.

Being on the forehand is not unusual for a horse who has recently been backed and has not yet learnt to adjust his balance to carry the rider with ease. Getting a horse off the forehand does not mean hitching him up with the reins so that he carries his head higher, it means getting him to engage more so that the hind quarters can carry an increasing proportion of the weight. This will entail building up the relevant muscles and teaching the horse to take his hind legs further under his body, so that they can carry more of the weight and lighten the forehand. Once again, it is those wonderful transitions that are the most effective way of putting the message across. However, it cannot be achieved overnight and, especially with young horses, getting a horse off his forehand should be looked upon as a gradual process.

On the forehand. The pony has not had much training and is not stepping far enough under with his hind legs. Most of his weight is on his forehand. This will make it difficult to manoeuvre him, to keep a balance and rhythm and to develop power.

HEAD TILTING

We often see horses (and riders!) going round with their heads on one side. The horses do this to help themselves remain balanced when they are not stepping forward evenly with both hind legs. Working on the hind quarters to get each hind leg thrusting forward with equal power is often the solution. Remember, too, that the uneven thrust may be caused by a rider who is sitting crooked and hindering the action on one side more than the other – so check your own position.

There is another possible cause, which is that when the rider asks for a flexion or bend with the inside rein, the horse lifts his chin instead of turning his head. In this case the horse needs to be made more supple through the poll so that he turns rather than tilts.

Head tilting. There is just a slight tilt developing, with the right ear lower than the left.

NOT WORKING THROUGH/NOT CONNECTED

Achieving the aim of the horse working through is not so easy, but it is the key to developing his athletic potential, and this is what makes dressage riding so much more exhilarating. The conditions necessary to make it possible (and thus those that need checking if your horse is not working through) are:

1)   A balanced, supple rider who can give clear, precise aids (see Chapter 5).
2)   A horse who is responsive to the aids (see Chapters 6 and 7).
3)   The basics established (see Chapter 8).

If your horse is not connected and working through it is usually easier to get him first into a pretty horizontal outline (but not on his forehand). In this position the muscles along the top line will find it easier to operate than if the horse is carrying his head and neck high. In trot, freshen up the pace; work in a larger area, making the horse go forward positively towards a contact with hands that are steady, elastic and tending towards a forward feeling.

CONCLUSION

If you want happiness for a lifetime help the next generation – Chinese proverb.

I hope that this book will help the next generation a little – and that it will give some indication of where to head and what fun it is to be heading there. Some will have plenty of help, ambitious parents, good horses or ponies, and abundant opportunities to train and compete; others will have to struggle, but they should not get disgruntled and jealous. Struggle is what makes more stars in the long run, rather than being handed everything on a plate. Remember – luck is not just the opportunity but recognising opportunity, being ready to seize and make the most of it. Whether you have an expensive trained schoolmaster or a shaggy pony, if you believe that he is the best horse in the world, and you are determined to maximise his and your ability, then you are going to get immense satisfaction out of dressage. You can gain as much pleasure from a judge giving you an 8 or 9 for a movement in a novice test, or leading the field in a Pony Club test, as you can from winning the European Championships. So go for it. Develop your horse's and your own potential and – whatever the standard – if you are getting anywhere close to maximising that potential, that is what dressage is about.

I have had my luck – such as being around to help Andrew Nicholson train for his first Olympics and playing a small part in turning Kristina Gifford from a not-so-hot dressage scorer on her Pony Club pony into a team World Three-Day Event Champion. But I have had as much satisfaction out of finding ways in which a Pony Club rider can turn a bumping into a sitting trot, or from seeing a seven-year-old do her first square halt. Working with the young, whether as a trainer or an administrator, is exhilarating and challenging, and I owe many thanks to those with whom I have been involved. Most of them have given me plenty of trouble – but also the stimulation and excitement of being with them when they embark on a trail that could lead to the Olympics, and that will certainly give them many character-building moments of glory and despair.

GLOSSARY

The following are some of the most common terms in dressage, and ones whose meaning might be difficult to work out from a dictionary.

Behind the vertical. Nose falls behind a vertical line running downward from the poll to the ground. It is a very common judge's comment as it is easy to spot and many horses work this way. It is a fault, but not a serious one so long as there is a positive, elastic, rein contact – in which case it is less serious than the other alternative of poking the nose out and up to come above the bit. When the horse comes behind the vertical because he is trying to avoid taking the contact then it bad fault.

Between leg and hand. This is a more vivid way of describing contact. When the rider's legs are used as driving aids, the horse steps forward more actively with his hind legs and the momentum is received in the roder's hand. The horse stays round and does not speed up or resist. His power remains between leg and hand. (See illustration on page 43.)

'Broken neck'. The arch of neck is not continuous from the wither to the poll. The horse bends his neck downwards three or four vertebrae back from the poll, so the poll is no longer the highest point.

Cadence. This is a pronounced rhythm. Cadence is the 'extra' that makes the paces special with the horse taking a definite moment of suspension in the trot and canter, the steps being well defined and the work marked by a pronounced rhythm.

Change the rein. The equestrian term for changing direction from clockwise to anti-clockwise or vice versa. To do this the rider will have to change the use of the reins, with the new outside rein to work towards and a new inside one to keep soft.

Connected. Literally means that the hind legs of the horse are connected to his mouth so that the impulse of a hind leg stepping forward and generating impulsion can be felt in the hand. It is similar in meaning to contact and between leg and hand. (See illustration on page 43.)

Contact. This is a rein contact with the bit (or mouth) which should be steady and elastic. The feature of this contact is that it is made by contact from the rider's legs and seat which encourage the horse to step forward, work over his top line and poll and so establish a contact with the hands. (See illustration on page 43.)

Counter-flexion. In most instances the horse is flexed to the inside of a circle, turn etc., but on some occasions in training it is useful to flex to the outside in a counter-flexion. This can help to loosen the horse and or position his shoulders more to the inside.

Counter-canter. As in counter-flexion it is usual in the canter to lead with the inside leg. The exercise of going around a corner with the outside leg leading is more difficult and is called counter-canter.

Disunited. This is when a horse changes leg in canter but only behind or in front. The result is that he leads with a different leg in front than behind and this is very uncomfortable.

Elasticity. The quality of a horse who is supple so that all his muscles are 'elastic', enabling him to spring softly forwards with each trot or canter step he takes, rather than appearing stiff or jerky in his movement.

Expression. (or Brilliance). This is a development of suppleness, balance and impulsion. Horses can be very obedient but make the work look rather flat and dull. What the judges and good riders are looking and training for are equine athletes who use all their body, who can spring off the ground, work with elasticity, and this is known as expression.

Fall onto outside shoulder. The direction of momentum generated by the hind legs is not directly forward towards the head, but diagonal, towards the outside shoulder from the inside hind which has drifted inwards. The weight will tend to fall onto that outside shoulder.

Flexion. The horse keeps his neck straight but turns his head from the poll and jaw so the rider can see his eye on that side.

Four-beat canter. The true three-beat is lost because the diagonal pair of legs hit the ground separately so four beats are heard.

Impulsion. This is contained power and not speed. It is the generation of energy from the hind quarters and this makes the movement of the horse more athletic.

Inside. The direction to which the horse is flexed or bent. The outside is the other direction, that is the side on which the horse is convex. This need not be the side which is on the out-side of the arena as, for example, in counter-canter.

Irregularity. When the horse loses the correct rhythm of the pace.

Leaning. The horse uses the reins as a prop, putting weight onto them, and the rider has to help support him. This is usually caused by the horse being on his forehand.

On the forehand. So much of the weight is falling onto the shoulders, neck and head of the horse that it will be difficult for him to stay balanced and keep in a rhythm. This is a natural state for the horse when first having to carry the weight of the rider, but a major objective of dressage is to make the horse more balanced; to carry more weight on his hind quarters; to step more under his weight with his hind legs so he can become lighter in his forehand, take lighter steps and become more manoeuvrable.

Outline/frame. This is the silhouette of the horse along his top line from the hind leg to his face.

Over-tracking. The hind feet step beyond the hoof prints of the forefeet (as in medium and extended paces).

Pace. The term for the gaits of the horse – the walk, trot and canter.

Pacing. Refers to the walk when it loses its correct four-beat and becomes two-time, with the legs moving in lateral pairs.

Quarters in. The hind legs do not step towards the forelegs but drift to the inside.

Quarters out. The hind legs do not step towards the forelegs but drift to the outside.

Round(ed). The neck appears to arch from the wither to the poll. The back is arched from the wither to the hind leg so the impression is of a rounded outline and taking round steps.

Self-carriage. This the result of well-engaged hind quarters and lightness of the forehand enabling the horse to carry himself – and in particular his head and neck – without having to balance himself on the reins. This carriage should be rounded, with the poll the highest point, and should be achieved by being balanced and not because the horse holds an outline through tightening and stiffening his muscles.

Short in the neck. The neck is compressed and contracted. The all-important arch to the neck with the top line stretched from the withers to the poll has been lost and the rider is usually holding the horse back with the reins.

Square halt. A balanced halt when the pair of forelegs are parallel and sharing an equal amount of the burden, as are the hind legs.

Tempo. This is the speed of the rhythm of the pace.

Through. This is the nearest one can get to the German word *durchlaessigkeit* which describes the horse's willingness to obey the aids instantly and without any resistance. The horse lets the rider's aids through without stiffening, resisting and tightening.

Tight back. The muscles in the back tighten so the horse cannot work through.

Tilting. The horse carries his head on one side so one ear is lower than the other.

Tracking-up. The hind feet step into or in front of the hoof prints of the forefeet (as is considered normal in working paces).
Wide behind. The hind legs are carried wide apart. This often happens in medium and extended trot, the horse tending to take his hind legs to the sides rather stepping forward under his weight.

Working from behind. The first step is with the hind leg, which is where the power is generated. The horse does not pull himself forwards by moving a foreleg first.

INDEX

ACKNOWLEDGEMENTS

I have really enjoyed writing this book. Because I wanted it to be simple and fresh, the work has been more spontaneous than any other book I have written. Fortunately, I have been able to call upon International Judges Joan Gold and Stephen Clarke to check sections of the manuscript and make helpful comments. I am most grateful for the contribution of their very special knowledge.

The photographs were taken at national and international events for the Under 21s, including the 1996 European Junior and Young Rider Championships in Copenhagen. Some young riders also helped with the training shots and my thanks go to the Smallman and Bechtolsheimer families, Kate Elliot and Timothy Heappey.

It is impossible to find or take photographs to portray all that one needs, and it has been wonderful to work with such a talented illustrator as Maggie Raynor.

Finally, I must thank Judy Kingham for her skills on the word processor.